William Randolph Hearst, Orson Welles, and *Citizen Kane:* The Men Behind One of America's Most Famous Movies

By Charles River Editors

About Charles River Editors

Charles River Editors is a boutique digital publishing company, specializing in bringing history back to life with educational and engaging books on a wide range of topics. Keep up to date with our new and free offerings with this 5 second sign up on our weekly mailing list, and visit Our Kindle Author Page to see other recently published Kindle titles.

We make these books for you and always want to know our readers' opinions, so we encourage you to leave reviews and look forward to publishing new and exciting titles each week.

Introduction

"Any man who has the brains to think and the nerve to act for the benefit of the people of the country is considered a radical by those who are content with stagnation and willing to endure disaster." – William Randolph Hearst

When William Randolph Hearst was in his late 50s and at the height of his power, journalist Robert Duffuss observed, "His career is unique in American history, or, for that matter, all history. Compared with him the Bennetts and even the Pulitzers are small…his acquaintances…credit him with personal charm, but do not deny his ruthlessness in business operations. Shopkeepers and his nearest rivals are simply not in his class. Here is success on a dizzying and truly American scale. Here is journalism as large as the Rocky Mountains or the Painted Desert."

However, despite his massive success, and perhaps in large measure because of it, many of Heart's contemporaries depicted him in negative ways. As Duffuss also noted, when it came to the newspaper magnate's reputation, there was "a curious suggestion of lath and plaster about it, and far from being universally honored and admired as other self-made men have been, Mr.

Hearst is regarded by multitudes of his fellow citizens with extreme aversion and distrust. Indeed, his career is almost never examined dispassionately and for this reason some of the salient facts about him are worth setting down in a somewhat cold-blooded manner."

It is only right to keep every positive and negative viewpoint in mind when looking at the life of a man who built his own fortune with money inherited from a father who literally grubbed it out of the ground with his own hands. While the senior Hearst may never have gotten the soil of old California from under his nails, William Randolph would never know what it felt like to live a life of manual labor; instead, he founded his empire on another kind of dirt, that which he was able to dig up and publish about the people, great and small, of his day. He would also stir up a good bit of dirt himself, living a high life with his mistress in California while his wife raised their children and did charitable work back in New York. Eventually, he would go too far, and nearly lose his empire when he backed Adolf Hitler over Franklin D. Roosevelt. By the time he died, it is fair to say that he had seen it all, done it all, bought most of it, and lost much of it. In spite of all this, he left behind an empire that continues to dominate the publishing business to this day.

When it comes to Hollywood and the entertainment industry, perhaps nobody catapulted to fame as quickly or as strangely as Orson Welles, and it was due in large measure to the man who hated him more than anyone else in the world. Though Welles he had worked on stage productions from an early age and seamlessly transitioned into radio, few were familiar with his work until a legendary 1938 radio broadcast of H.G. Wells' *The War of the Worlds*, during which some people who heard Welles narrating the work truly believed that an alien invasion was underway. As Welles famously apologized at the end of the broadcast, "This is Orson Welles, ladies and gentlemen, out of character, to assure you that The War of the Worlds has no further significance than as the holiday offering it was intended to be; The Mercury Theatre's own radio version of dressing up in a sheet and jumping out of a bush and saying 'Boo!'"

Although the alleged widespread hysteria caused by that broadcast is mostly overstated, the notorious broadcast made Welles a household name, and he only followed it up with one of the greatest movies ever made: *Citizen Kane*. As the co-writer, producer, director, and main star of the film, a biting social critique of William Randolph Hearst, Welles' first movie would end up being his most famous and critically acclaimed. Of course, it also ensured that he would continue to work across every entertainment medium for the next 4 decades, juggling radio, the stage, movies, and television throughout the rest of his illustrious career.

William Randolph Hearst, Orson Welles, and Citizen Kane: The History of the Men Behind One of America's Most Famous Movies examines the various roles Hearst played in American journalism and politics during his life, and how he "inspired" Welles to make one of America's most important films. Along with pictures depicting important people, places, and events, you will learn about the story of Hearst, Welles, and *Citizen Kane* like never before.

Building a Publishing Empire

William Randolph Hearst was born on April 29, 1863, to newlyweds George and Phoebe Apperson Hearst. His father, as he was always proud to say, was a pioneer who came to California during the Gold Rush and made and lost a number of fortunes throughout his lifetime. His mother was even more unique, an independent woman who at 19 agreed to marry the 41-year-old George, but only after receiving certain considerations. On June 14, 1862, the day before they were married by a local minister, the two signed and registered the following prenuptial agreement at the Crawford County Courthouse in Steelville, Missouri: "This marriage contract made & entered into this 14th day of June, 1862 between, George Hearst of the one part & Phebe E. Eperson [sic] of the other part both of the County of Franklin & State of Missouri "to wit." The parties to this instrument in consideration of the covenants & stipulation hereinafter mentiones promises & agrees to intermarry with each other within a reasonable and convenient time after the execution hereof. 2. The said George Hearst in consideration of said future marriage hereby for himself conveys assigns & sits over unto the said Phebe E. Eperson Fifty Shares of stock in the Goaldine & Curry Gold and Silver Mining Company of Virginia City Nevada Territory U.S. out of this interest which said Hearst had in said Mining Company to be held for & during the natural life of said Phebe E. Eperson and at her death revert to the said George Hearst his heirs or legal representatives."

George Hearst

Phoebe Hearst

When William was born, Phoebe assumed that he would be the first of many children. With that in mind, as well as the cultural norms of the mid-19th century, she left Willie, as they called him, with a nurse while she continued on with her own pursuits. According to Hearst biographer David Nasaw, "For the next twenty years, George and Phoebe Hearst would be apart far more than they would be together. Both, if we can believe their letters, suffered from the arrangement, but Phoebe had the more difficult time, at least at first. George was at home in the West and had become accustomed to the predominantly male world of the mining camps. Phoebe was new to the West, new to city life, and a young mother."

At the same time, it seems that George truly loved his young wife and cared about at least her physical comfort. In early 1864, Phoebe and Willie moved into an elegant new home on Chestnut Street in San Francisco purchased for them by George, but they made the move on their own as George remained at mining camps hundreds of miles away. In addition, she was about to lose her parents, who themselves were moving to a farm near Santa Clara (also purchased by

George).

In order to focus on the move, Phoebe sent Willie with his nurse, Eliza Pike, to Santa Cruz in early June. During this separation, Phoebe wrote many letters to Eliza, many filled with angst and drama that reflect the flightiness of a young mother barely out of her teens: "It seems a month since you left. I am terribly lonely, I miss Baby every minute. I think and dream about him. We all feel lost…I have had another letter from Mr. Hearst…he expects to be home soon, but don't say what he means by soon, a week, or a month…Kiss Willie for me and write me how he is. I hope you will wean him…I am going to telegraph Mr. Hearst to know what to do about moving up on the hill, we have only two weeks more. I don't think I can come down to see you I will be so very busy. Write often. I feel anxious to hear from you. Oh dear what am I going to do."

In time, Phoebe grew into her new role, and Nasaw noted that, with George gone so much, "Phoebe adjusted to life as a single mother. She learned to make decisions by herself, run the household, and raise Willie. She was assisted of course by her husband's wealth, which provided her with a household filled with servants and the incentive and leisure to educate herself - and her boy."

As time passed and no other children came along to join her growing son, she became quite a doting mother, and one who some might characterize as obsessive. In 1871, Phoebe wrote to a friend, "I take great pleasure in amusing and interesting him at home so that he may be kept as much as possible from bad children. Of course, I must allow him to have company often but I manage to watch them closely. So far he is a very innocent child and I mean to keep him so just as long as I can…He is a great comfort to us. Mr. Hearst is so proud of him and too indulgent to try to keep from spoiling him…Mr. Hearst often says he would not like to have Willie on a jury if his Mama was concerned, for whether it was justice or not, he would decide in my favor…I am so sorry we have no other children. We love babies so dearly, why we are not blessed I cannot understand…I have had the dressing room adjoining my bedroom all fixed up for Willie, a nice bed put up. It is a pretty little room and so near me, he is very much pleased."

Two years later, when he was still just 10 years old and had only been in school for two years, Phoebe removed young Willie from school again to take him on an extended trip to Europe. While the trip itself would obviously be extremely educational for an impressionable young child, Phoebe also arranged for him to have regular lessons in all his academic subjects. With that said, her motivation for taking him does not seem to necessarily have been his best interests as much as her own need. From her letters, it becomes clear that, while George and Phoebe Hearst had a very good marriage, she needed nearly constant companionship and often turned to her son for company when her husband was working the long hours needed to support them and improve the family's circumstances.

As it turned out, the family's fortunes took a downturn during the Panic of 1873, while Phoebe and Willie were in Europe, and when they returned home in October 1874, George, at Phoebe's suggestion, had sold their home on Chestnut Street. The family would spend the coming years in one rented space after another, even though their circumstances were always quite comfortable.

By this time, George Hearst was known on the West Coast as both an outstanding prospector and excellent judge of mining properties. He certainly enjoyed gambling both in business and for pleasure, though not in excess. In the mid-1870s, he accepted a small newspaper called the *San Francisco Examiner* as a payment of a gambling debt a friend owed him, and he would pass this company on to Willie about a decade later, setting in motion his son's rise to publishing royalty. All the while, the sense of instability brought on by moving from place to place and school to school may have led the younger Hearst to develop a passion for acquiring material possessions that would mark the rest of his life.

As the son of a wealthy and prominent man now involved in state and national politics, it was important to his family that the only Hearst heir receive an excellent education, one that was not available to him in California. Thus, his parents shipped him off across country to be educated in New England. After finishing a tenure at St. Paul's School in Concord, New Hampshire, Hearst enrolled in Harvard College in 1880. According to a 1951 article published in *The Harvard Crimson*, "During his three College years, Hearst had an opportunity to display some of the publishing talent that later built the greatest newspaper empire ever known in America. His field of activity was modest--the Harvard Lampoon. He took over as business manager of the funny magazine when it was laboring under heavy arrears of debt, and in two years transformed it into a paying proposition." George Santayana, who also served as an editor of the *Lampoon*, remembered, "The fact that his father was a millionaire and a Senator from California gave him an independence that disturbed the undergraduate mind, and his long cigars were bad form in the Yard. Yet his budding prowess as a newspaper owner and manager made him invaluable to the Lampoon in its financial straits."

The article also made reference to one of Hearst's less noble acts, one that may have led to his early departure from college. Hearst expressed his interest in collecting art too early and too casually, and his gifts to several professors of their visages etched on the bottom of chamber-pots proved that Harvard did not have the West's sense of humor. Young Hearst was invited to leave Harvard a year before graduating, and returned to California in disgrace.

Once back home, Willie's mother made sure that he suffered no serious repercussions for his lapses, even while his father insisted that he had to find something useful to do with his life. After drifting along for a couple of years, in 1887 Hearst persuaded his father (who by that time had become a U.S. Senator from California) to make him the editor of the *Examiner*. Writing a few decades later, journalist Robert Duffuss observed, "Everyone knew that a youngster like this was certain to make a failure of newspaper work, and it was his father's newspaper which he had chosen for his plaything. There was even reason to suspect that the Senator himself entertained few delusions on the subject. The only question was how long the money would last and what toy the amateur editor would take up next when the varnish had worn off this one."

Hearst soon proved them wrong, and with near unlimited funding from his parents, he made sure the "Monarch of the Dailies" had the best of everything, from equipment to writers. He also began to publish stories that sought to uncover both private and political corruption.

Among those he brought on board to investigate the shady dealings was a somewhat notorious author who had already demonstrated his journalistic skills in other California papers. Writing on September 4, 1889, Ambrose Bierce held readers in the palm of his hand as he observed some inconsistencies present in a local murder trial: "Redwood City, the town from which Mr. Powell thought it expedient to remove Editor Ralph Smith, has the distinction and advantage of numbering among its "prominent citizens" two brothers named Ross, one of whom is an ornament to the legal profession; the other adorns the medical. At the time when Mr. Powell sated his desire for the absence of Editor Smith by shooting him down in cold blood when he was unarmed, the medical Ross held the office of coroner and naturally conducted an inquest with a view to ascertaining if anyone was in fault. The post mortem examination showing that only two of Mr. Powell's bullets had penetrated the body, and that only one of these had done any damage…seems to have convinced Dr. Ross, the coroner, that Mr. Powell's connection with the matter was too slight really to implicate him in a murder; for he straightway went upon his bail bond…Possibly Dr. Ross may have been able more clearly to discern his duty to go upon Mr. Powell's bail bond by the broad beam of revelation thrown upon that gentleman's innocence by Lawyer Ross' retention for the defense. The Ross blood is apparently a good deal thicker than water—thicker even than the blood of poor Ralph Smith, upon the hands of Mr. Powell." Bierce concluded, "We cannot, of course, say with certainly whether Ross was influenced by fraternal considerations in standing by his brother's client; his belief in Mr. Powell's blameless intentions in shooting down an unarmed and comparatively weak man and shooting him after he was down…may sufficiently account for his act. To accuse such a man of fraternal feeling, or feeling of any kind, is going pretty far." Needless to say, this type of hype sold papers, and the *Examiner* was soon among the most popular papers in San Francisco.

With the money he was now making, Hearst decided to build himself a home of his own near Pleasanton, California, though it must be noted he built the home on land owned by his father and his mother ended up taking over the project. Nonetheless, it was still his home, and he named it Hacienda del Pozo de Verona. Writing for *Diablo* magazine in 2006, Susan Davis vividly described the estate: "[Phoebe's] husband bought the 500-acre property in 1886 but died shortly thereafter, in 1891. William Randolph then started to convert the ranch house on the property into a hunting lodge. Hearst feared that her son was going to use it to entertain his rough friends, so she took over the project. She also wanted more than a hunting lodge. A long-time supporter of women's advancement, she hired Julia Morgan, the first female architecture student at the prestigious Ecole des Beaux-Arts in Paris and the first licensed female architect in

California. It would take more than a decade to complete Hearst's mansion, but it ended up being one of the most magnificent homes in America. Hacienda del Pozo de Verona was named after a 15th-century carved-stone wellhead (pozzo means well in Italian) that William Randolph had shipped from Verona, Italy. The house was a showcase from the moment a visitor stepped into its large entry courtyard and was greeted by the sight of the ornate wellhead serving as a large fountain. Inside, Hearst exhibited her massive collection of artwork and furniture, as well as artifacts from around the world that she picked up on her travels…The main building was three stories and had more than 50 rooms. One of the fireplaces was large enough to spit-roast a whole ox. The estate's playhouse, designed for Hearst's five grandchildren, rose two stories high and contained 13 rooms, billiard tables, and several reading rooms. The list of guests over the years included royalty, artists, composers, presidents, and movie stars from far and wide."

Hearst did not live in his new home for long. As an ambitious young man, California was only the beginning. The way he saw it, San Francisco, and even all of California itself, was too small a territory for him, so he soon turned his attention east and began to dream of owning multiple newspapers stretching across the country. With Phoebe's emotional and financial backing, Hearst purchased the *New York Morning Journal* in 1895. As he had with the *Examiner*, Hearst poured money into these establishments, hiring such prominent authors as Julian Hawthorne and Stephen Crane to write the kind of sensationalized stories made popular by the current king of journalism, Joseph Pulitzer. Not surprisingly, Pulitzer took umbrage at Hearst, especially when the newcomer stole his best illustrator, Richard Outcault. As the two entered into an all-out war for readership, Hearst slowly lured away many others from Pulitzer's staff, causing the older man no end of stress and misery.

Pulitzer

Crane

Among the many ways in which Hearst managed to outdo Pulitzer was in how he treated his employees. Writing in *The Uncrowned King: The Sensational Rise of William Randolph Hearst*, Kenneth Whyte pointed out, "Hearst quickly established himself as the most attractive employer on the street, and a clear favorite over the suspicious and volatile Pulitzer, his chief rival for newspapering talent. Journalists responded with dedication and enterprise. They followed their proprietor's lead in subordinating all other concerns—office politics, administrative niceties, sobriety—to the overarching goal of creating a great and popular newspaper. And the Journal, effectively a new publication without a preexisting style or personality, quickly found its voice."

As he built up his reputation for being a fair and reasonable boss, Hearst was able to lure away several of Pulitzer's best editors, including Morrill Goddard, who was responsible for building interest in the growing American pastime of reading the Sunday paper. He also brought over a young man named Arthur Brisbane, who was already on his way to becoming one of the most important newspaper columnists in American history. Hearst made Brisbane the managing editor of the business.

Hearst, Robert G. Vignola, and Brisbane in 1920

In 1896, a popular trade paper, *Printer's Ink*, quoted a local advertising executive as saying, "I cannot help feeling that that man Hearst had struck it. He has done what he alone could have done. The success is as conspicuous, as mysterious, as actually present as the electric light. It is here, we see it, we know it, and it is Hearst that has done it. He has created a great property and it will grow and grow. He alone had done it. It was not his money…It was not the men he has gathered around him…but the success is attributable solely to him…." The executive in question continued, "Nothing succeeds like success, and it is upon…a phenomenal success that the young man from the other side of the continent is already rearing a colossal structure—upon a foundation already plainly seen to be wide and broad and strong enough to sustain any weight and height its projector may aspire to construct. He will do what…has not been done." Perhaps the secret of Hearst's success could be found in his paper's motto: "While Others Talk, the

Journal Acts."

Due to issues related to copyright, both the *World* and the *Journal* ran a comic series drawn by Outcault and called the *Yellow Kid*. According to one expert, the series "presented a turn-of-the-century theater of the city, in which class and racial tensions of the new urban, consumerist environment were acted out by a mischievous group of New York City kids from the wrong side of the tracks…Americans embraced the Yellow Kid during a time when commerce became central to the American way; the comic grew popular on the pages of two of the leading newspapers, and even influenced another 'clean' newspaper editor to name the papers' explicit reporting of New York City urban life 'yellow-kid journalism.'" The term stuck, and it was shortened over time to "yellow journalism," especially around the time of the Spanish-American War.

It wouldn't be possible to definitively determine who was most responsible for the radical changes that newspapers made near the end of the 19th century and the beginning of the 20th century as they transformed themselves into something like modern tabloids instead of traditional, dry sources of news. Pulitzer certainly started the trend, and he had been publishing such stories since Hearst was still in school, but Hearst, in his quest to beat Pulitzer at his own game, upped the ante, cashing in by exaggerating run-of-the-mill stories to sell papers. Ironically, as Kenneth Whyte noted, some of the sensationalism actually served the public well in some instances: "It is true that news of society and calamities were a part of the paper's formula for success. They were a part of every major Park Row daily's formula for success. … Hearst, in fact, improved the quality of crime and disaster coverage at the *Journal*. He engaged readers less with frights than by illuminating character and creating narrative by playing up the arts of police detection and courtroom argument, by delineating justice issues and moral controversies and vigoruously taking sides in them. He made similar improvements to the paper's gossip and society news, eliminating a clutch of cheesy columns with names like 'Gossip of the Swells' and the 'Jolly Joker,' in favor of Alan Dale's popular reviews and 'Caught in the Metropolitan Whirl,' a smart new column containing short, breezy observations about city life. The whole paper was being reworked. The quality of its prose, while still uneven, was improving steadily. The design, on the whole, was more polished. Coverage was more comprehensive throughout: foreign and financial news were expanded, along with sports and arts."

A picture of the *New York Journal's* coverage of the murder of Stanford White in 1906

Unable to beat Hearst at telling gripping stories, Pulitzer decided to cut his prices, reducing the cost of his papers from two cents to a penny, the price Heart charged, and before long, both men were willing to do nearly anything to outsell the other.

While newspapers today are accused of being partisan, those in the 1890s were unabashedly so, and the *Journal* was no different. Hearst made it clear that any publication with his name on it would be a populist paper, thereby supporting the more liberal principles of the Democratic Party. In fact, the *Journal* was the only major newspaper on the East Coast to back William Jennings Bryan's run for the presidency. Hearst made it his business, and that of his reporters, to ferret out any and all examples of graft or corruption in the campaign run by Republican candidate William McKinley. The most important story his team uncovered concerned Mark Hanna, who had carved out for himself a place as the first political "boss" to gain power across the nation, whereas others, such as the infamous "Boss Tweed," had merely attained local influence. According to Hanna biographer David Croly, "For a while [Hearst reporter Alfred] Lewis appears to have been stationed in Cleveland in order to tell lies about him. He was depicted as a monster of sordid and ruthless selfishness, who fattened himself and other men on the flesh and blood of the common people. This picture of the man was stamped sharply on the popular consciousness by the powerful but brutal caricatures of Homer Davenport. Day after day he was portrayed with perverted ability and ingenuity as a Beast of Greed, until little by little a certain section of public opinion became infected by the poison. Journals of similar tendencies elsewhere in the country followed the lead with less ability and malignancy but with similar persistence. … As the scope of his political activity increased, the approbation which he wanted and needed had to come from a widely extended public opinion. Hence…he could not but wince under a personal distortion which was at once so gross and brutal, and yet so insidious and so impossible to combat…this concentration upon his own person of a class hatred and suspicion wounded and staggered him, until he became accustomed to it, and was better able to estimate its real effect upon public opinion."

Hearst profited from the attacks and their effectiveness, so much so that the post-election edition of the *Journal* broke all previous sales records by topping 1.5 million copies. He had owned the paper for barely a year.

Hearst is probably most famous – or infamous - for his involvement in getting the United States involved in the Spanish-American War. The Cuban Revolution of 1895 came at an ideal time for Hearst, who had just purchased the *Journal* and was looking for a way to make a name for himself on the East Coast. When the Cuban rebels declared their independence from Spain, their demands resonated with Hearst and many other Americans, and before long, the *Journal* was regularly promoting the rebels' cause by publishing articles and cartoons that portrayed the rebels as innocent victims of repeated atrocities by the Spanish.

Time and again, Hearst called upon the American government to intervene on behalf of the Cuban rebels, and he also made sure his reporters were always on the prowl for a scoop. They were even encouraged to become personally involved in events. In one of the most provocative stories of the era, reporter Karl Decker learned of a beautiful 17-year-old girl being held in a Spanish prison for supposedly inciting rebellion. Her name was Evangelina Cossio y Cisneros, and Decker was determined to obtain her freedom. He first tried to do so by bribing guards to let her out, and when that failed, he used his influence to persuade a Cuban dentist and an American businessman to break her out. The three took a ladder to the jail under the cover of darkness, climbed up to her window and managed to loosen enough bars in the decaying walls to free her. They spirited her away to the United States, where she gave the *Journal* exclusive access to her story.

Evangelina Cossio y Cisneros

In situations like these, rumors crop up that often last for generations. One of these involved a message that Hearst supposedly sent the famed artist Frederick Remington, who was then working for him as an illustrator. Hearst had sent Remington to Cuba to cover the fighting, but Remington cabled back to him that there was no fighting to cover, and that he wanted to return to America. According to legend, Hearst cabled back, "You furnish the pictures. I'll furnish the war."

W. Joseph Campbell, author of *Yellow Journalism: Puncturing the Myths, Defining the Legacies*, has questioned whether this actually happened, writing, "Reasons for doubting [James] Creelman's anecdote are many. They go beyond Hearst's denial, made in 1907 and repeated in the autobiography of one of his sons. They go beyond the fact that the telegrams Creelman described have never surfaced. … Searches of Remington's papers produced no reference to his purported exchange with Hearst. But the correspondence of Davis, the most prominent American war reporter of the time, offers telling evidence that the exchange never happened. In one letter, Davis said Remington left because he had 'all the material he needs for sketches and for illustrating my stories.' In a more expansive letter, Davis said he asked Remington to leave because Davis disliked 'traveling in pairs.'"

    According to a 1998 *New York Times* article, "Many of the reporters who covered the Cuban uprising had front-page ink on their minds, not ethics…Hearst even sent a ceremonial sword with a diamond-studded ivory handle as a gift to General Maximo Gomez, commander of the Cuban rebel forces. An intrepid cub reporter, Ralph D. Paine, volunteered to present the sword to the rebel leader to get his first big scoop." Even those who were trying to keep clear of the drama often found themselves caught up in the media frenzy, as the *Times* noted in relaying the story of the well-respected foreign correspondent Richard Harding Davis: "Unwilling to get caught up in the hype, he left Cuba on the mail steamer Olivette without asking permission from his editors at The *Journal*. While steaming home, he met a young Cuban woman named Clemencia Arango, who was expelled by General Weyler as a suspected guerrilla collaborator. She told Mr. Davis that she had been repeatedly disrobed on the orders of Spanish detectives searching for secret messages to Cuban exiles in Tampa. Mr. Davis wrote about the woman's ordeal, but buried it in a longer piece. When his editors got down to the undressing part they saw red meat, and had Mr. Remington draw an illustration of a young woman, her naked rear end showing, forced to strip before Spanish agents. The *Journal's* headline read: 'Does Our Flag Shield Women?'" The article concluded, "Reporters following up on the story later learned that the Spanish agents had used matrons to do the undressing, and, as proper gentlemen, they never viewed the woman's naked body themselves. No matter; she became a cause celebre for the war hawks."

Remington

Davis

Despite leaders hoping to stay above the fray, American economic interests were being harmed by the ongoing conflict between Cuban nationalists and Spain, as merchants' trading with Cuba was suffering now that the island was undergoing conflict. Furthermore, the American press capitalized on the ongoing Cuban struggle for independence, which had been flaring up time and again since 1868. In an effort to sell papers, the press frequently sensationalized stories, which came to be known as yellow journalism, and during the run-up to war, yellow journalism spread false stories about the Cuban conflict in order to sell newspapers in the competitive New York City market.

President McKinley wished to avoid a war, but he was forced to support a war with Spain after the USS *Maine* suffered an explosion in Havana's harbor in February 1898. McKinley had sent the ship to help protect American citizens in Cuba from the violence that was taking place there, but an explosion rocked the ship, which had to be towed to harbor and eventually scuttled. That took place only after 266 American sailors aboard the ship were killed.

No sooner had the men landed on American soil in Key West than they were besieged by questions about what they believed had happened on their ship. To their credit, most were reticent and discreet in their speculations. John Blandin noted, "I have no theories as to the cause of the explosion. I cannot form any. I, with others, had heard the Havana harbor was full of torpedoes [mines], but the officers whose duty it was to examine into that reported that they found no signs of any. Personally, I do not believe that the Spanish had anything to do with the disaster. Time may tell. I hope so. We were in a delicate position on the *Maine*, so far as taking any precautions was concerned. We were friends in a friendly, or alleged friendly port and could not fire upon or challenge the approach of any boat boarding us unless convinced that her intention was hostile. I wish to heaven I could forget it. I have been in two wrecks and have had my share. But the reverberations of that sullen, yet resonant roar, as if the bottom of the sea was groaning in torture, will haunt me for many days, and in the reflection of that pillar of flame comes to me even when I close my eyes."

Within just a few days of the explosion, American divers arrived to explore the ship's wreckage and file a report on what they saw. They were also there to try to recover as many bodies as they could. One recalled, "It was horrible!…As I descended into the death-ship the dead rose up to meet me. They floated toward me with outstretched arms, as if to welcome their shipmate. Their faces for the most part were bloated with decay or burned beyond recognition, but here and there the light of my lamp flashed upon a stony face I knew, which when I last saw it had smiled a merry greeting, but now returned my gaze with staring eyes and fallen jaw. The dead choked the hatchways and blocked my passage from stateroom to cabin. I had to elbow my way through them, as you do in a crowd. While I examined twisted iron and broken timbers they brushed against my helmet and touched my shoulders with rigid hands, as if they sought to tell me the tale of the disaster. I often had to push them aside to make my examinations of the interior of the wreck. I felt like a live man in command of the dead. From every part of the ship came sighs and groans. I knew it was the gurgling of the water through the shattered beams and battered sides of the vessel, but it made me shudder; it sounded so much like echoes of that awful February night of death. The water swayed the bodies to and fro, and kept them constantly moving with a hideous semblance of life. Turn which way I would, I was confronted by a corpse."

Photo # NH 46774 Diving on MAINE's wreck

Less than a month after the *Maine* went down, the United States Navy convened a board of inquiry to determine the cause of the explosion. Other than some sort of outside attack, the only other explanation, given the strength and location of the blast, was that some sort of fire broke out on the ship and detonated something flammable.

While authorities were trying to investigate the causes, New York's papers immediately tried to get out in front of each other with wildly speculative accounts, all of which blamed the Spanish. As Jim Squires noted, "Press responsibility was a big issue then, too. Pulitzer and his imitator/rival, William Randolph Hearst, were accused of starting the Spanish-American War with their unsupported and arguably irresponsible accusations that Spain had blown up the U.S. battleship Maine in Havana harbor. And the sleaziness of their juvenile public feud over a comic strip character called 'the Yellow Kid' spawned the infamous term 'yellow journalism,' which still lives today. Meanwhile, circulation doubled at Pulitzer's *World* to 800,000, tripled at Hearst's fledgling *Journal*, and newspapers in general were soon transformed from a small, elitist enterprise appealing to commercial and political interests to a medium for the masses. For the first time, immigrants had to learn how to read English just to get by."

A picture of the headline in the *New York World*, which belied the fact that Pulitzer privately conceded "nobody outside a lunatic asylum" should believe Spain was responsible

The headline in Hearst's *New York Journal*

Over 115 years later, the explosion of the *Maine* is perhaps best remembered for being associated with yellow journalism and as the primary cause of the Spanish-American War, which makes it somewhat fitting that the explosion itself remains an unsolved mystery. There was never another official public investigation carried out by the American government after 1911, but several private investigations have sought to answer the enduring mystery, and the most recent efforts have theorized that the explosion was an accident caused by burning coal. A 1974 investigation led by Admiral Hyman G. Rickover was the first major study to suggest that a spontaneous combustion of coal in one of the ship's bunkers triggered the explosion of an adjacent magazine, which then caused the heavy majority of the damage.

Ultimately, the loss of the USS *Maine* drew America into the war, and in that endeavor, McKinley and the federal government were given a shove from Hearst. As the *Times* noted a century later, "The first story in Pulitzer's New York World carried a banner headline that left little doubt about who was responsible: 'Maine Explosion Caused by Bomb or Torpedo?' The Journal published a diagram of what it called a secret 'infernal machine' that struck the ship like a deadly torpedo -- apparently the figment of some journalist's imagination."

When the United States finally declared war in 1898, Hearst personally traveled to Cuba to get a front row seat for the fighting. Chartering a yacht to live on while he was there, he ran the "Cuban Edition" of the *Journal*, making sure that his readers learned of extra gory detail of the battles, especially of any stories glorifying the rebels or vilifying the Spanish.

To be fair, Hearst was not merely out to sell newspapers; he did, in fact, believe in that the Cuban rebels were justified in their struggles. Spain had indeed been cruel in its treatment of the Cubans, and had executed hundreds of thousands of those who opposed them. Like Pulitzer, Hearst knew his audience well, and he never doubted that his readers would respond to the stories he told of these injustices. Those men covering the war for Hearst knew the importance of getting their stories, and two of them, Edward Marshall and James Creelman, were injured during the fighting. When the war was finished, General Calixto Garcia, the head of the Cuban rebels, presented Hearst with a bullet-riddled flag in recognition of his support for the rebel cause.

The war only lasted a few months, but it was long enough for Hearst to get a sense of his power in the nation, and he was not about to back down from telling the government what it ought to do. He continued to be a man whom politicians were wise to fear, for the *Morning Journal* was selling more than a million issues a day by the time the Spanish-American War started. In spite of this, Hearst continued to lose money on his publishing venture, perhaps as much as $1 million a year in his first few years in business. This was because, while he was selling plenty of papers, his prices were too low, so that he could continue to undercut Pulitzer. However, with the war over, the men were able to call a truce, and the *World* and the *Journal* stopped actively competing with each other in 1898.

No longer focused entirely on beating out Pulitzer in New York, Hearst was able to expand his interests nationally. In the early years of the 20th century, he established newspapers in cities as diverse as Boston and Los Angeles, as well as Chicago. Hearst biographers Oliver Carlson and Ernest Sutherland Bates, writing in the mid-1930s, explained some of the hardships these maneuvers entailed: "The establishment of a new paper in Chicago was not an easy matter in those days, especially when the invader was as dangerous as Hearst was recognized to be. The rival papers hired thugs to run his newsboys off the streets. But such methods were not likely to terrorize an heir of the San Francisco vigilantes. Hearst hired more thugs than his enemies and ran their newsboys off the streets. When thug met thug, a fine battle would ensue. Teamsters and delivery men joined the holy war on behalf of their masters, until traffic became so disrupted that the police at last interfered to restore law and order. It was evident that Hearst had come to stay. How well he had mastered the methodology for such crises was shown years later when the Hearst papers in San Francisco employed identically the same means to keep Cornelius Vanderbilt out of their field."

Hearst also remained heavily involved in national politics, regularly denouncing President William McKinley, in his editorials, including one in which he declared, "If bad institutions and bad men can be got rid of only by killing, then the killing must be done." He quickly regretted using such harsh language and dispatched Creelman to the White House to make amends. According to Creelman, "Mr. Hearst offered to exclude from his papers anything that the President might find personally offensive. Also he pledged the President hearty support in all things as to which Mr. Hearst did not differ with him politically. The President seemed deeply touched by this wholly voluntary offer and sent a message of sincere thanks."

Creelman

McKinley

Despite the olive branch, Hearst soon resumed his attacks on McKinley, and when McKinley was assassinated shortly after being reelected, many in the nation were incensed. In fact, some subsequently asserted without any evidence that Hearst's writing had inspired the assassin. Following McKinley's death on September 14, 1901, the Grand Army of the Republic, still held in the highest esteem for the Civil War, resolved, "That every member of the Grand Army of the Republic exclude from his household 'The New York Journal,' a teacher of anarchism and a vile sheet, unfit for perusal by any one who is a respecter of morality and good government."

McKinley's successor, President Theodore Roosevelt, also took up the cry. During his first message to Congress in December 1901, he insisted, "When we turn from the man to the Nation, the harm done is so great as to excite our gravest apprehensions and to demand our wisest and most resolute action. This criminal was a professed anarchist, inflamed by the teachings of professed anarchists, and probably also by the reckless utterances of those who, on the stump and in the public press, appeal to the dark and evil spirits of malice and greed, envy and sullen hatred. The wind is sowed by the men who preach such doctrines, and they cannot escape their share of responsibility for the whirlwind that is reaped. This applies alike to the deliberate demagogue, to the exploiter of sensationalism, and to the crude and foolish visionary who, for whatever reason, apologizes for crime or excites aimless discontent."

The King of His Castles

In an attempt to mitigate at least some of the considerable damage done to his reputation and that of his paper, Hearst changed the name of the *Morning Journal* to the *American* after McKinley's death. He also considered running for public office himself, no doubt hoping to punish Roosevelt for his cutting words. In public, of course, he cast running for office as a moral, civic duty, claiming, "My early ambition was to do my part in newspapers, and I still propose to do a newspaper part. But when I saw mayors and governors and presidents fall, I felt that I'd like to see if I couldn't do better. I felt I'd like to go into office, any office almost, to see if I couldn't do the things I wanted to see done." According to Carlson and Bates, what Hearst really believed was that a "political office, any office almost, could be a stepping-stone to the presidency, but that some political office was a prerequisite."

Thus, Hearst set about on his own political career. Carlson and Bates explained, "Hearst chose the easiest and most available, that of representative from the Eleventh Congressional District of the City of New York, an office entirely under the control of Charles F. Murphy, the reigning boss of Tammany Hall. The publisher's decision to enter politics was opposed by most of his friends. There was still a journalistic tradition, more honored in the breach than the observance, that an editor should be independent of political parties, and should never sacrifice this independence by becoming a candidate for office. The experience of the one prominent journalist who had gone into politics, Horace Greeley, vainly seeking the presidency and dying of chagrin after his defeat, was not such as to encourage imitation. But Hearst knew that he should not die, and his determination remained unshaken."

Hearst launched his campaign on October 6, 1902, telling an audience gathered to hear his first political speech, "I believe that of the eighty millions of people in this country, five or six millions (the most prosperous five or six millions) are ably represented in Congress, in the law courts, and in the newspapers. It would be immodesty on my part to imagine that I could add much to the comfort or prosperity of the few who are so thoroughly well looked after. My ambition is to forward the interests of the seventy millions or more of typical Americans who are not so well looked after. Their needs seem to offer a wider field for useful effort. At the same time let me say that I do not seek to divide the nation into classes or foster unreasoning dislike of one class by another. I can recognize and admire the genius and the generosity of the great captains of industry…My interest is in the average American citizen. The welfare of the country demands that he too shall secure a fair share in the advantages of prosperity…" Hearst won his election easily.

Now nearly 40 years old, Hearst decided to get married and settle down. However, much to the chagrin of his closest friends, he eschewed the many suitable daughters of New York society and instead married a 21-year-old vaudeville dancer named Millicent Willson. The two were married on April 28, 1903 and immediately left for an extended honeymoon in Europe.

Millicent Hearst

These were hardly the actions of a committed politician, but then, there was nothing to suggest Hearst was all that committed to his political career. In fact, Carlson and Bates noted, "No congressman ever took his legislative duties more lightly than did Congressman Hearst. He rarely attended the meetings of the House, and when he did, he voted still more rarely. During the first and second sessions of the Fifty-Eighth Congress, which were continuous from November 9, 1903, to April 28, 1904, he responded to the roll-call but nine times."

With that said, Hearst did champion a handful of bills, including the following list:

"an amendment to the Interstate Commerce Act, giving the Interstate Commerce Commission the power to fix railroad rates;

an amendment to the Sherman Anti-Trust Act designed to strengthen it;

an inquiry relative to alleged railroad combinations in the transportation of anthracite coal;

a bill to appoint a committee for the investigation of trusts;

one to establish a parcel post system; another to regulate towing at sea."

As Carlson and Bates concluded, "All of these were enlightened measures…And, once having introduced his resolutions and seen them referred to the appropriate committees, where nearly all died a natural death, Hearst took no further interest in them save to give the impression through his newspapers that he was an exceedingly active congressman."

In spite of his relatively paltry record and lax participation, Hearst won reelection. He ran for the presidency in 1904, but he was unable to secure the Democratic nomination. After that, he turned his sights to the New York City mayoral race in 1905, which he lost. He then lost his bid to become New York's governor in 1906. He ran for mayor again in 1907, this time as a member of the Municipal Ownership League, a political party he established himself. He lost again.

When Hearst ran for mayor again in 1909, the whole thing had become something of a running joke. As one writer not so delicately put it, "During the ten years William has been active in New York State politics, he has been identified with more parties as a candidate or a promoter of candidates of his own personal selection than any other man in fifty years. At one time or another he has been the regular party candidate of two parties — the Democratic and Independence League, or Independence party, as it later became known. He has openly fused with the Republicans on two occasions, once in promoting the candidacy for sheriff of Max F. Ihmsen, his campaign manager for several years, and with the Republican organization then in control of former Governor Odell in 1903 to elect. He has been active in both the major political parties and has twice operated a party of his own. He has frequently been a candidate for office; with the exception of one inconspicuous term in the lower House of Congress, these ambitions have not met with success at the polls anti-Tammany candidates to the board of aldermen. In the present campaign he has fused with the Republicans to the extent of hitching on to all the candidates nominated by the regular Republican organization with the exception of mayor."

Perhaps not surprisingly, Hearst's experiences led to his disenchantment with politics. Looking for something new to excite his interest, he spent the next several years expanding his business empire. Already owning a number of newspapers, Hearst purchased two news services, and he molded one of them into the *International News Services* in 1909. Decades later, it would merge with the *United Press* to become the now famous *United Press International*.

During this period in his life, Hearst joined many other men of his age and station in becoming fascinated by the emerging aviation industry. It all began in January 1909, when a French pilot, Louis Paulhan, took him up on his first flight. In an article published on January 22, 1910 in *The*

Editor and Publisher, Hearst breathlessly described the experience, writing, "We left the commonplace of this worn-out world behind us, beneath us, and lifted into a new life, into a new era. The sensations of flying are difficult to describe, for the human mind operates through analogy and is convinced by comparisons, and there is nothing with which to compare the sensations of flying. I felt that great sense of exhilaration which all aviators describe, and in addition a deep serenity, a calm enjoyment of what seemed to be the perfect conditions of a new and better state. The little people below, growing littler, too, every moment, seemed to belong to the past, to a period when men walked miserably upon the face of the earth or rolled uncomfortably in primitive autos over the rough surface. We…were of the new era; we were soaring gloriously through space; we were flying. As a matter of fact, M. Paulhan was doing the flying and I was merely holding on. and quite tight, too, but I felt altogether as grand and superior as he could possibly have felt."

In 1910, Hearst established the Hearst Transcontinental Prize of $50,000 (more than $1 million today) to be given to the first pilot to fly from one coast to another in fewer than 30 days. No one managed to accomplish this feat before the prize expired in November 1911, but in the years that followed, he sponsored *Old Glory*, a Fokker F.Vlla single-engine monoplane, in a failed attempt to cross the Atlantic. It would take more than another decade for Charles Lindbergh to accomplish that feat.

While maturity moved Hearst away from sensationalizing stories, he never lost his boyish interest in cartoons, and throughout his career he hired and promoted some of the most talented artists of the era. Among them was George Herriman, who in 1913 invented a strip called *Krazy Kat*. While it initially made only a minimal stir in the publishing world, Hearst stood by it and kept it running for decades, insisting it was a classic. It was only after the comic ended in 1944 that many critics acknowledged he was right.

Herriman

A *Krazy Kat* cartoon

Anxious to consolidate and protect the copyrights of his popular comic strips, in 1914 Heart founded King Features Syndicate as a single corporation owning all his syndicated features. Within two years, King Features had carved a niche for itself in the newspaper business, bringing on staff members to create and draw new material that it could in turn sell to newspapers across America. During the years of the Great Depression, the company provided features to more than 13,700 newspapers.

Politically, Hearst remained a populist, but he became steadily more interested in isolationism than in any other issue. In a 2016 article for *The Atlantic*, writer Eric Rauchway spelled out some of Hearst's activities and stances during World War I: "Before the United States entered World War I, Hearst's sympathies lay with Germany. He used his publishing empire to gather pro-German editors and writers around him, did a deal with a German agent for newsreel footage, and used a paid agent of the German government as his newspaper correspondent for German matters. But once the United States declared war on Germany, Hearst could no longer maintain this stance, so he took up a new one. With American flags decorating his newspapers' masthead, he declared that the freshly belligerent Americans should tender no aid to the Allies also fighting Germany: '[K]eep every dollar and every man and every weapon and all our supplies and stores AT HOME, for the defense of our own land, our own people, our own freedom, until that defense has been made ABSOLUTELY secure. After that we can think of other nations' troubles. But till then, America first!' Wilson had used 'America first' to position the United States as an international leader; Hearst interpreted the slogan to mean preserving, in sympathy with the Germans, above all and absolutely the security of the American homeland and the American people. Hearst's version stuck, not least because he revived it to oppose the 1932 nomination of Franklin Roosevelt for president and to invent the candidacy of John Nance Garner." Hearst remained pro-German and anti-Wilson in the years following the war, and he stringently opposed the president's vision for the League of Nations.

Already enamored with the burgeoning movie business, in 1915 Hearst established an animation studio called the International Film Service. Animation was an easy business to break into for Hearst since he already owned many of the most popular comic strips in the United States. A few years later, in 1918, he partnered with Paramount tycoon Adolph Zukor to form Cosmopolitan Pictures in New York City. The deal benefitted both men, as Zukor was given first refusal for the rights to make movies from stories featured in Hearst's many magazines. At the same time, the members of the public who had already read the stories or merely heard of them were essentially a preexisting audience that would likely be anxious to see the film. Naturally, the Hearst magazines would help with promotion by publishing articles that publicized the movies.

What most Americans did not know (and most likely would not want to know) was that Hearst's reasons for creating Cosmopolitan Pictures were at least as personal as they were practical. Now in his early 50s, Hearst appeared to be a devoted husband and proud father of five growing sons: George Randolph, born in 1904; William Randolph, Jr., born in 1908; John Randolph, 1910; and twins Randolph Apperson and David Whitmire, born in 1915. However, the supposedly settled businessman had fallen in love with a 20-year-old showgirl named Marion Davies.

Unlike most relationships involving married men and mistresses in the early 20th century, Hearst was devoted to Davies from the start, and he remained committed to her for the rest of his life. She wanted a career in movies, so he created a movie studio that would cast her without any questions. Writing for *Slate* magazine in 2015, Karina Longworth explained, "In 1918 Hearst signed Davies to a contract with his newly-formed production company, Cosmopolitan Pictures, at $5 a week. Davies had a stutter, but that didn't matter—she had big, expressive eyes, highly photogenic blonde hair, and an adorable pout. Even Davies' detractors would have to admit that she was incredibly photogenic, and she could sell a joke. Davies' memoirs reveal the actress to have a dry sense of humor, above all about herself. As she would crack about her career beginnings, 'I couldn't act, but the idea of silent pictures appealed to me because I couldn't talk either.' Hearst's stroke of genius when it came to Marion Davies was to use what he had already proven had worked…If he wanted something to happen, he would report that it was happening, and then it would happen. And so Hearst put the weight of his newspaper empire into spreading the news about this amazing new star, Marion Davies, and then he found some movies for her to star in. By 1920, Davies had appeared in seven films…"

Marion Davies

As a wealthy man with both a wife and a mistress, Hearst believed he needed a new home where he and Davies could live together, away from disapproving eyes. To this end, in 1919, he began work on what would come to be known as Hearst Castle. Located on his ranch near San Simeon, California, which sprawled across over 240,000 acres, Hearst Castle would become the center of life and entertainment for many celebrities on the West Coast in the years to come.

Historian Jana Seely offered a virtual tour of what guests could expect at Hearst Castle: "All the guests at San Simeon occupied rooms furnished with the works of art accumulated by Hearst. They slept in sixteenth-century beds, kept their clothes in seventeenth-century chests of drawers, and watched fires burning beneath five-hundred-year-old mantels…One of the ways William Randolph Hearst ensured others' enjoyment of art was by enlivening mundane domestic items with antique components. Hearst residences were furnished not only with fine antique mantels, but also with antique fireplace equipment such as andirons, pokers and grates. Wrought-iron candlestands were transformed into floor lamps, marble columns were used as sculpture pedestals, iron grilles protected windows, and architectural elements such as ceilings were frequently incorporated into the very fabric of the building, often augmented, sometimes altered, by the work of Hearst craftsmen…This intense interest in a wide range of objects not traditionally sought by the other great collectors is one of the factors that sets William Randolph Hearst apart and contributes to his reputation as something of a maverick. His purchases included doorknockers, warming pans, tile stoves, musical instruments, pipes, and lanterns in addition to mainstream art such as paintings, sculpture, tapestries and silver."

Needless to say, everyone wanted to be invited to "the Ranch," as Hearst called it, and during the 1920s and 1930s, he and Davies hosted one decadent weekend party after another. Hearst made sure that the estate was always easy for his guests to reach, even those who could not fly in in their own planes and land at the estate's on site airstrip. For these less fortunate guests, Hearst provided a private train car that they could take from Los Angeles. Those arriving were typically left to their own designs during the day, but at night they could expect to meet anyone from Clark Gable to Winston Churchill around the dinner table. Franklin D. Roosevelt stayed over early in his career, as did Bob Hope and Cary Grant. Charlie Chaplin might be seen complaining about the impact of talking pictures on the movie industry, while Charles Lindbergh praised the rising Third Reich. After dinner, guests were often invited to view a first run movie, from Cosmopolitan Studios, of course, in the estate's private theater.

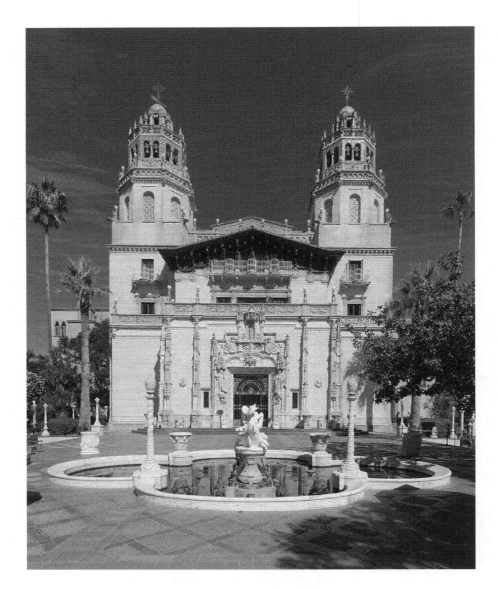

A picture of Hearst Castle

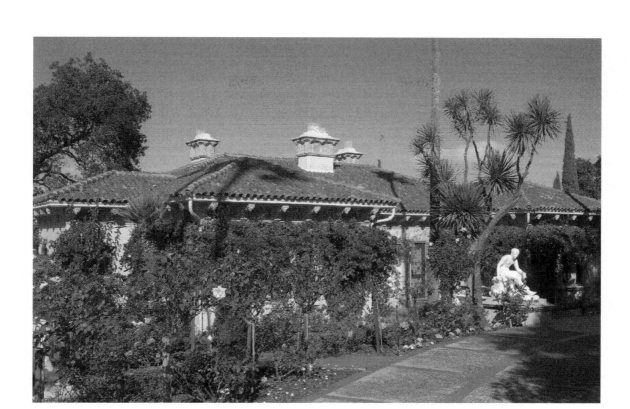

One of Hearst Castle's guest houses

Bernard Gagnon's picture of the Hearst Castle dining room

For times when he did not wish to entertain, or to do so in an even more private setting, Hearst could retreat to his estate on the McCloud River in Siskiyou County, California. Called Wyntoon after a local group of Native Americans, it had been built by his mother in 1902. So enamored was Hearst of the Bavarian style mansion that he used the same architect, Julia Morgan, to design Hearst Castle. However, Phoebe did not leave the estate to Hearst when she died in 1919, instead willing it to her favorite niece, Anne Flint. Determined not to lose the home his family had enjoyed for years, Hearst immediately began to scheme to get the property back, and in 1925 he purchased it from Flint for just under $200,000.

Hearst was acquiring everything he wanted, and he was bearing the brunt of the publicity surrounding his relationship with Davies, but that still had ramifications for everyone else involved. Longworth observed, "it was common knowledge that Davies was Hearst's mistress. … The Catholic Hearst hadn't divorced his wife, Millicent, and he never would—but Davies would live with Hearst openly for decades." This all but ensured nobody would take Davies' movies seriously, though Longworth pointed out that Davies was actually "fun, funny, and liked by just about everyone, and other papers were starting to take notice of Davies' beauty and vitality, particularly after the 1921 film Enchantment, in which Davies played a flapper a full two years before…the flapper type's on-screen debut."

Davies in *When Knighthood Was in Flower* (1922)

Ironically, Hearst disapproved of such vapid roles, determined that this modern girl he was living with should behave off stage in the same manner in which his wife and mother conducted themselves. As Longworth noted, many believed "it was exactly their non-conventional relationship that made Hearst so intent on protecting Davies' persona. Hearst knew he and Marion could never marry, and because of that he knew that she would always be considered by many to be a fallen woman, living in sin. In insisting that she never lose her quote-unquote dignity on screen, Hearst was in a sense trying to restore the virtue he had felt he had robbed from her in life."

Over the next few years, Hearst kept pouring virtually unlimited resources into Davies' career. Longworth continued, "In February 1923, Hearst found a distribution partner for his production company in Goldwyn Pictures. A little more than a year later…Goldwyn's assets were brought into [Metro-Goldwyn-Mayer], including…their contract with Hearst, which meant that Davies and her movies were now de facto property of MGM. Hearst went on to negotiate an unprecedented deal for himself and Marion, who he had named president of his Cosmopolitan

Pictures in order to ensure that she would get a sizable share of the profits, and have money of her own. Under the MGM deal, the studio fully financed the movies, and turned 30 percent of the profits over to Hearst and Davies, who was also paid a salary of $10,000 a week, of which MGM paid 60 percent and Hearst paid the rest…In exchange for financing and distributing Marion's movies, MGM had unlimited access to Hearst publications for the promotion of its films." This was an important consideration, and it likely smoothed Davies' way when it came to talking pictures, but no matter how much talent she had, her professional life was always overshadowed by her relationship with Hearst.

   It was during this period that Hearst made one of his most unusual purchases in the form of St. Donat's Castle in Vale of Glamorgan, Wales. He first saw the property in an issue of *Country Life Magazine* in 1907 but never forgot it. Ultimately, he bought the castle in 1925 and began restoring it as a gift for Davies. Together, the two traveled throughout Europe, spending exorbitant sums to purchase entire rooms for themselves that they found in other castles. Hearst even bought the Great Hall, guest house, tithe barn and Prior's lodging from Bradenstoke Priory in England and had them dismantled and moved to St. Donat. He had the Great Hall completely rebuilt and used materials from the other buildings to create a banqueting hall at St. Donat's. Updating the structure, he added 34 bathrooms to accommodate the needs of his many guests. Each had fixtures made entirely of green and white marble.

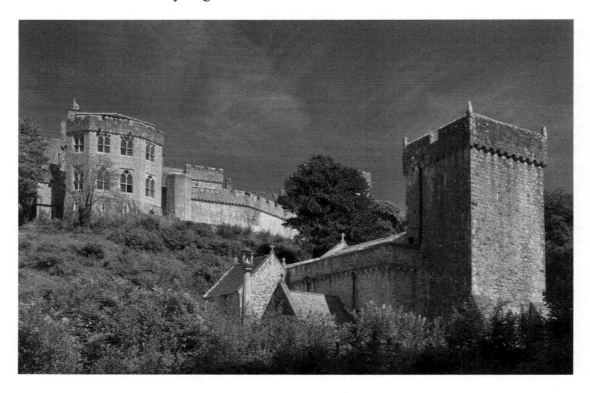

Mick Lobb's picture of the castle from its courtyard

No matter what else he was doing, Hearst was always first and foremost a newspaper man, and while he was often dogmatic on issues concerning American politics, he was not so certain or committed when it came to his attitudes concerning other countries. In some cases, this worked to his credit, such as when he initially supported the Bolshevik Revolution when it began in Russia in 1917 but turned against the communists as the unrest and bloodshed spread. If there was any steadfast principle, it was that Hearst generally opposed American involvement in any overseas conflict, or even peacekeeping efforts, such as those proposed by Wilson for the League of Nations.

By the time the Roaring Twenties were in full spring, Hearst was one of the most influential men in America. He owned 28 newspapers across the country, from the *Seattle Post-Intelligencer* to the *Washington Times*, and he had also expanded his interests into publishing books and magazines, including such still popular periodicals as *Good Housekeeping* and *Harper's Bazaar*. His most controversial publication, however, was the *New York Daily Mirror*, a tabloid he launched in 1924. In the decade that followed, Hearst would have a mixed relationship with the broadsheet, selling it in 1928 and then buying it back in 1932.

In addition to promoting papers and movies, in the late 1920s Hearst also became more interested in air travel. In 1929, just months before the stock market crashed and he lost much of his fortune, Hearst spent a sizeable sum of money sponsoring the airship LZ 127 Graf Zeppelin on its famous voyage around the world. The voyage began at the Naval Air Station at Lakehurst, New Jersey, which would become known for being the site of the famous Hindenburg disaster. The ship returned to Lakehurst just three weeks later.

While he would likely never admit it, Hearst's fortune was never entirely his own, and at many turns, newspaper empire did not always break even. He had long been dependent for capital on the fortune his father had created, which meant the Great Depression drove many of his publications out of business. He made his losses worse by publicly opposing President Roosevelt's efforts to change the country's economic direction. Roosevelt was a popular man, and many of his supporters refused to buy papers that criticized him. Eric Rauchway noted, "Hearst…stepped forward in January [1932] with a speech decrying the internationalist Roosevelt as a Wilsonian meddler, opportunist, and the sort of fellow who would 'allow the international bankers and the other big influences that have gambled with your prosperity to gamble with your politics.' Hearst preferred 'a man … whose guiding motto is "'America First,'"." and named Garner—the Texas congressman who had, for slightly less than a month, been speaker of the House—as that man. Garner did not then know he was the leading anti-Roosevelt candidate for president or that, as an inveterate free-trader, his motto was 'America First.' Hearst, unfazed, hired a campaign biographer to invent a log-cabin birth and other suitable prerequisites for Garner, whose appeal, as one observer noted, was as 'a Democratic Coolidge'—or, as Garner himself said, someone who believed 'the gravest possible menace' facing the country was 'the constantly increasing tendency toward socialism and communism.' Here, he was reciting a verse from the Hearst hymnal."

Film historian Deborah Carmichael observed, "Hearst...brought his political message to millions of moviegoers in 1933 with his Cosmopolitan Films' production of "Gabriel Over the White House." Collaborating with scriptwriter Carey Wilson, Hearst himself wrote some of the politically charged oratory of President Hammond (Walter Houston). It is quickly revealed that President Hammond, a pleasure-loving and pliable politician, has gained the presidency through the support of party leaders. These leaders remind him regularly of the many favors he owes them. He answers to political shysters and not the American people suffering through the Great Depression. After a life-changing event...this fictional president experiences a spiritual and political epiphany guided by the archangel Gabriel.... A transformed President Hammond, who now resembles Abraham Lincoln physically and spiritually, acts rapidly to rid the nation of an unseen enemy--rum-running gangsters. Invoking his position as commander in chief, he adjourns Congress, disbands his Cabinet, institutes martial law, and after conviction by a military tribunal, orders death by firing squad in the shadow of the Statue of Liberty for the bootleggers who have threatened the stability of the country. Hammond further eliminates domestic problems by forming a CCC-like program. He gets foreign debts repaid by bullying world leaders with a display of military might. The problem of returning to a constitutional government is neatly solved as Gabriel, an angel of both vengeance and mercy, kills off President Hammond, who returns to his former self after completing the rescue of his country."

In a move he would come to regret, Hearst also started publishing articles written by the rising German leader Adolf Hitler. He praised Hitler for opposing the spread of communism and for focusing his attention on improving his own country. Hearst felt that Hitler's style of nationalism was something Americans could learn from, apparently seeing no problem with the fact that Hitler was notorious for encouraging his followers to beat up anyone who opposed the Nazis.

When Roosevelt won the Democratic nomination in 1932, Hearst used all the influence he could muster to force Roosevelt to choose John Nance Garner as his running mate. Pleased that Roosevelt did so, Hearst supported him in his run and for the first few months he was in office. However, Roosevelt's plans for the New Deal were too liberal and too radical for the son of a self-made millionaire, and Hearst ultimately went after him with all his might. Rauchway explained, "With 'AMERICA FIRST' at the center of his newspaper masthead, emblazoned above a stylized eagle clutching a ribbon reading, 'AN AMERICAN PAPER FOR THE AMERICAN PEOPLE,'...Hearst now saw communism everywhere—not only in the Roosevelt administration, but among college professors 'teaching alien doctrines' and among striking union workers in San Francisco, against whom Hearst's papers encouraged vigilante violence."

Once again, Hearst had seemingly changed his political stripes. According to biographer Ben Proctor,: "During the 1920s he became an avowed Jeffersonian Democrat, warning his fellow citizens against the dangers of big government, of unchecked federal power that could infringe on the individual rights of Americans, especially if a charismatic leader was in charge....[After supporting FDR in 1932] Hearst soon became highly critical of the New Deal. With increasing frequency Hearst newspapers supported big business to the detriment of organized labor. With unabated vigor they condemned higher income tax legislation as a persecution of the "successful."""

By 1937, Hearst was teetering on the edge of financial ruin. A quite unflattering article published on July 9 of that year told readers, "One by one reactionary newspapers are finding surcease in the journalistic boneyard—victims of the own publisher's personal hatred and stupidity. Two Hearst owned papers, the Rochester Herald and the New York American, recently have suspended publication. The American, for many years the most powerful paper in the Hearst chain, had been losing ground for several years and it known to have lost its owners a cool million last year." The article concluded sardonically, "Newspaper dictatorship, as exemplified by some of the metropolitan dailies, like political dictatorship, is bound to run its course. Sooner or later public opinion will make itself felt."

While some may have sympathy for Hearst's losses related to his political beliefs, he made plenty of business and personal mistakes that also contributed to his downfall. For one thing, he always had a difficult relationship with blue collar workers, and he often suffered at the hands of strikes organized by trade unions. He also failed to keep up with the changing times and fell behind new competitors, such as the *New York Daily News*, that thrived during this time. When money became tight, he refused to economize, instead purchasing more expensive art pieces for his collection and mortgaging San Simeon for $600,000 to pay for his lifestyle. When Joseph P. Kennedy, Sr. a rising millionaire, politician, and patriarch of the Kennedy political dynasty, offered to buy Hearst's magazines, he refused to sell.

Kennedy

On top of it all, Davies' film career was tanking, and most of the movies Hearst made lost money.

In an attempt to dig himself out of the financial hole he was in, Hearst eventually parted with an extensive part of his art collection. These sales are perhaps the only reason the public ever learned just how much money he had tied up in his collection. In 1937 alone, he sold off more than $11 million, which bought him some relief, but he still had to sell another 20,000 items, including paintings, chalices, croziers, windows and pulpits from ancient churches, a sideboard once owned by Charles Dickens, and Thomas Jefferson's Bible, as well as a waistcoat that had belonged to George Washington. Even after these sales, his collection still filled his various residences.

The War of Two Worlds

"We're born alone, we live alone, we die alone. Only through our love and friendship can we create the illusion for the moment that we're not alone."

George Orson Welles was born in Kenosha, Wisconsin on May 6, 1915, and his family was already plenty familiar with the Midwest; his father, Richard Hodgdon Head Welles, was from Missouri, while his mother, Beatrice Ives, was from Illinois. Richard named his son after his own grandfather and great uncle, Orson and George Head, and by the time his son was born, Richard had made a fortune by patenting a new type of bicycle lamp that had proven very popular. This allowed Beatrice to live a comfortable life and devote herself to her music.

The Welles' were a wealthy family and respected in Kenosha, but they were not without troubles. Their oldest son, "Dickie", was in an institution due to a mental disability, and Richard was such an alcoholic that by the time young Orson was 4 years old, his father was no longer able to work. At that point, the family left their home in Kenosha to move to Chicago, but the couple took up separate residences, with Beatrice supporting herself and her son by playing the piano at the Chicago Art Institute. A few years later, when Orson was 9, Beatrice died of hepatitis in a local hospital.

Before her death, Beatrice taught Orson to play the piano, but when she died, so did his interest in music. His father was still unable to care for him, so Dudley Crafts Watson, a professor with whom Beatrice had worked, took the boy in. Though the family lived in a big comfortable home called "Trillium Dell" on Marshman Avenue in Highland Park, Orson was not happy there. When he was 10, he and the Watsons' young daughter Marjorie both ran away, and when the Watsons found the two a week later, they were performing for money on a Milwaukee street corner.

Shortly after the Watsons took the children home, they enrolled Orson in the Todd School for Boys in nearby Woodstock, and they retained informal guardianship over the boy until he was 15, when Richard died and Dr. Maurice Bernstein took their place. For his part, Welles never got over his father's death, due in large measure to the fact that the adults taking care of him had persuaded him not to visit Richard until he quit drinking. So when he died, Orson later recalled, "[T]hat was the last I ever saw of him…I've always thought I killed him…I don't want to forgive myself. That's why I hate psychoanalysis. I think if you're guilty of something you should live with it."

Although he had a troubled upbringing, Welles enjoyed his years at the Todd School. Roger Hill, the headmaster, had no background in teaching and thus took a very modern, flexible approach toward education. He also took the sensitive boy under his wing and allowed him an unusual level of academic freedom to study the subjects he was most interested in. Given the way his career turned out, it's not surprising that Orson joined the school's travelling dramatics team, the Todd Troupers, and by the time he was 13, the troupe made him their artistic director.

Later, Welles and Hill would create Everybody's Shakespeare, a series of special adaptations of the Bard's plays designed to interest high school students. Not only did Welles believe that everyone could understand Shakespeare, he also believed that no one else would ever reach his genius (though Welles would certainly try): Welles explained, "He wrote all the plays that we need. And he knew it. He knew it. He wrote a short verse in which he said that nobody would match him. He was apparently an enormously charming man. Nobody ever spoke against him. Everybody loved him. And what's interesting are the new discoveries about his acting career, that he probably played much bigger parts than we had heretofore thought."

After he graduated in 1931, Welles won a scholarship to Harvard University, but while this might have been a dream come true for most young men, Welles was unimpressed. As he later put it, "I finished high school in two years and had a scholarship to Harvard. I hated school! Hated school! The trouble with school is that it's very good for some minds, and very bad for others. It is giving you opinions. All the time, opinions about history, opinions about people, opinions about everything. Goals are opinion factories. So I went into the theater so as not to go to Harvard!"

Instead of heading to Harvard, Welles took some of the money he inherited from his father and decided to use it to travel to Europe, which included a wonderful walking trip through Ireland. Not only did the visit give Welles a chance to hone his painting skills, it also gave him a chance to try his hand at some "off-stage" acting. One day, while visiting Dublin, he slipped into the Gate Theatre and asked to see someone in charge. He then told the manager, Hilton Edwards, that he was a star on America's Broadway stages.

By this time, Welles was over 6 feet tall and weighed about 200 pounds, with big brown eyes and a distinct speaking voice that his friends could recognize anywhere, so even though he was not a good enough actor to fool Edwards, he was self-assured and good looking enough to get his attention. Edwards allowed Welles to audition for a part in their 1931 production of *Jew Suss*, and Orson got a lead part as the Duke, as well as other smaller parts that made a big splash on the Dublin stage. He remembered his first professional role years later, saying, "My biggest success was with Jew Suss, the first flight I ever did. In Dublin."

In fact, Welles was such a big hit that word of his triumph made it back to the United States even before he did, but he was not ready for so much attention, so instead of trying out for more stage roles, he moved back to Woodstock to work at the Todd School. Once he went back there, he and his former headmaster Hill edited the plays in Everybody's Shakespeare for publication, renaming it The Mercury Shakespeare, and the series would sell more than 100,000 copies over the next decade and remain in print for most of the rest of the 20th century. While working on the Shakespeare project, Welles also continued to travel, including a trip to North Africa to work on pen and ink drawings for illustrating the books.

In 1933, Welles met Thornton Wilder, a popular New York playwright, and Wilder took a liking to the young man. He encouraged Welles to try his hand at the American stage, so in 1933, Orson joined Katherine Cornell's company and toured the East Coast with three off-Broadway productions, including Romeo and Juliet. For a while, it seemed that at least one of the shows would eventually open on Broadway, but when that didn't happen, Welles became discouraged and moved back to Woodstock, where he organized a drama festival at the Todd School. Not only did he lure a number of important Broadway actors to the school, but in a true coup for that era, he persuaded Hilton Edwards to fly to the United States from Ireland to appear at the festival.

Ultimately, the festival was a huge success, and it brought Welles to the attention of some distinguished people in the entertainment world. One of these was Paul Stewart, an actor turned director, who introduced Welles to another director, Knowles Entrikin. Entrikin subsequently offered Welles a job with The American School of the Air, an education radio show airing each week on CBS, but even though Welles was happy to have a job, his heart lay elsewhere. During this time, he shot his first film, the eight minute long *The Hearts of the Age*, at the Todd School. In the film, Welles played opposite actress Virginia Nicolson, whom he later married on November 14, 1933.

Orson and Virginia

For the rest of his life, Welles would have a difficult time reconciling his love for both the theater and motion pictures. He would once confess, "Films are either superior to or inferior to the theater. The battle between the two will always exist. The lack of live actors will always be to the advantage of movies and to its disadvantage. There are things you can do in movies that require the absence of live actors. Therefore, it is a more versatile media. But the theater, which requires live actors, can achieve things that films can never reach, because what's up on the screen is dead. It's only an image – there are no people there. Nobody who didn't see him in the theater will ever know how great W.C. Fields was. He was a shadow of himself in films."

At the time, however, Welles went to work in Manhattan, acting on air with people who would become lifelong friends. In 1936, John Houseman hired Welles to work for the Federal Theatre Project of the Works Progress Administration (WPA), a New Deal program created to give Depression Era performers work. He assigned Welles to the Negro Theater Unit, where Welles promptly began production on *Voodoo Macbeth*, a version of the classic Shakespeare tale set in Haiti. Jack Carter starred as Macbeth, and the play opened in Harlem on April 14. It became so wildly popular that it eventually went on tour across the nation, , and when one of the lead actors later fell ill, Welles himself took his place. This era in Welles' life obviously shaped his thinking, leading him to one day declare, "Race hate isn't human nature; race hate is the abandonment of human nature."

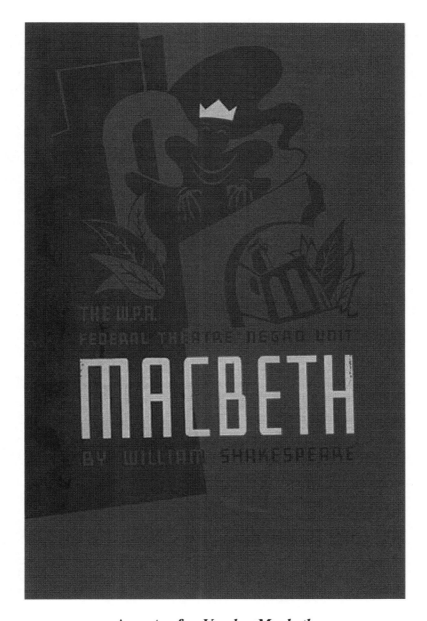

A poster for *Voodoo Macbeth*

Still only 20 years old, Welles was already highly praised as a directing prodigy, and he followed his *Voodoo Macbeth* success with *Horse Eats Hat* in the fall of 1936 and *The Tragical History of Doctor Faustus* in early 1937. Welles would later say of *Horse Eats Hat*, "The farce Horse Eats Hat was the best of the Mercury shows — and, though successful, it divided the town. The press was mixed, yet it was always packed, and had an enormous following. Some people went to it every week as long as it ran."

Later in 1937, Welles also directed *The Second Hurricane* with newcomer Aaron Copland, who would go on to become a renowned composer, and Welles also hired a young actor named Joseph Cotten for $10. The two would go on to work together on many productions in future years.

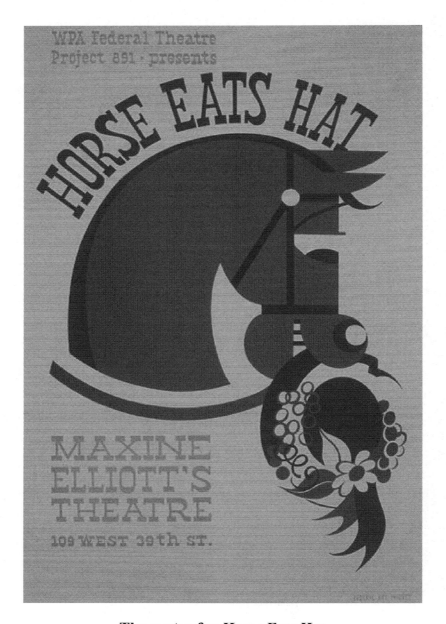

The poster for *Horse Eats Hat*

In the spring of 1937, Welles began work on *The Cradle Will Rock*, a political satire that angered some of the leaders of the WPA so much that they cancelled its opening at the Maxine Elliott Theatre and even posted guards to keep everyone out, including the cast itself. To save the production, Welles arranged for those who were willing to move to the Venice Theatre 20 blocks away, so the show went on for two weeks.

In spite of that, Welles remained a loyal supporter of Franklin Roosevelt and his policies. In fact, he never blamed Roosevelt for closing the theater, believing that the problems stemmed from those outside the White House, and he would always speak well of Roosevelt on his radio show. Welles would go on to campaign for the president's reelection in 1944. Nonetheless, Welles was also determined to be independent from further censorship, so he and Houseman teamed up to form the Mercury Theater in New York. Welles was the executive producer, and as such he was able to work with such great names of the era as Agnes Morehead, Ray Collins and Erskine Sanford. Their first play was a modern-day take on Julius Caesar set in Fascist Italy, and the death of Caesar was so well done that on opening night the audience applauded the scene for 10 minutes straight.

Never one to sit still, during the second year that the Mercury Theater was open, Welles directed a version of *Hamlet* on CBS's The Columbia Workshop, and in July 1937, he produced a seven-week long series based on *Les Miserables*. This eventually led to the creation of the Mercury Theatre On the Air, a weekly hour-long show that aired on CBS for 22 weeks, in the summer of 1938. Welles later praised the radio, saying, "Radio is what I love most of all. The wonderful excitement of what could happen in live radio, when everything that could go wrong did go wrong. I was making a couple of thousand a week, scampering in ambulances from studio to studio, and committing much of what I made to support the Mercury. I wouldn't want to return to those frenetic 20-hour working day years, but I miss them because they are so irredeemably gone."

As it turned out, one of the Mercury Theatre On the Air broadcasts would become arguably the the most legendary radio show in American history. By October 1938, Welles had been producing the show for a few months and had gotten positive reviews of his episodes, which had focused on such classics as *Oliver Twist* and *Treasure Island*, but with Halloween coming up at the end of the month, he wanted to do something special for the holiday. As a result, he decided to air a dramatized version of H.G. Wells' *The War of the Worlds*, but the production followed the sci-fi thriller by featuring a number of "news bulletins" that cut into an ongoing radio program and announce that Earth was being invaded by aliens from outer space. Even before production, CBS's censors had made changes to the broadcast because it sounded "too realistic", including changing the names of actual locations in the U.S.

Mindful of the particular problem, Welles announced on air before the program started that it was a dramatization of Wells' *The War of the Worlds*, but this didn't do much because American listeners, then as now, often cut back and forth between two programs, in this case the popular Edgar Bergin/Charlie McCarthy comedy program that aired on another channel at the same time. As a result, some people tuned in to Mercury Theater in the middle of the performance and heard bulletins announcing that aliens were attacking New York City and people were "falling like flies" across the city. The future *Tonight Show* legend, Jack Paar, later recalled that people were calling into the CBS affiliate studio in Cleveland where he was working and that he had to assure them, "The world is not coming to an end. Trust me."

Similar kinds of panicked calls took place elsewhere, and listeners flooded police stations with pleas for information about what was going on. Some of these stations, themselves in the dark about the broadcast, added to the panic by passing concerns up the chain of command. As one Welles biographer, Frank Brady, noted, some who started listening in the middle of the broadcast mistook the invading aliens for Adolf Hitler's Germans: "For the entire month prior to *The War of the Worlds*, radio had kept the American public alert to the ominous happenings throughout the world. The Munich crisis was at its height. Adolf Hitler, in his address to the annual Nazi party congress at Nuremberg in September, called for the autonomy of the Sudetenland, an area on the Czech border regions populated by three million Sudeten Germans, as they were called. Hitler ranted and lied over German radio … For the first time in history, the public could tune into their radios every night and hear, boot by boot, accusation by accusation, threat by threat, the rumblings that seemed inevitably leading to a world war."

Welles was aware of the potential for fooling listeners, and he even timed some of his bulletins based on when competing radio shows would take a break or end. That said, in addition to the disclaimer at the beginning of the show, he also included one at the end: "This is Orson Welles, ladies and gentlemen, out of character, to assure you that *The War of the Worlds* has no further significance than as the holiday offering it was intended to be; The Mercury Theatre's own radio version of dressing up in a sheet and jumping out of a bush and saying 'Boo!' Starting now, we couldn't soap all your windows and steal all your garden gates by tomorrow night, so we did the next best thing. We annihilated the world before your very ears and utterly destroyed the CBS. You will be relieved, I hope, to learn that we didn't mean it, and that both institutions are still open for business. So goodbye everybody, and remember please for the next day or so the terrible lesson you learned tonight. That grinning, glowing, globular invader of your living room is an inhabitant of the pumpkin patch, and if your doorbell rings and nobody's there, that was no Martian, it's Halloween."

Nevertheless, the chaos that resulted literally became the stuff of legends, and even the subject of more than one documentary, including 1975's Television docudrama *The Night That Panicked America*. People have been debating the actual extent of the program's influence on listeners ever since, and Welles himself subsequently hyped up the effects of the broadcast on listeners: "Houses were emptying, churches were filling up; from Nashville to Minneapolis there was wailing in the streets and the rending of garments."

While it's clear that some people were confused enough to try to call police stations and newspaper offices to try to verify the broadcast, most scholars dismiss the suggestion that there was widespread panic. As one South Dakota man wrote to the Federal Communications Commission, "I was one of the thousands who heard this program and did not jump out of the window, did not attempt suicide, did not break my arm while beating a hasty retreat from my apartment, did not anticipate a horrible death, did not hear the Martians 'rapping on my chamber door,' did not see the monsters landing in war-like regalia in the park across the street, but sat serenely entertained no end by the fine portrayal of a fine play."

Most importantly of all, even if the notorious broadcast didn't cause hysteria across the nation, it made Orson Welles famous.

Citizen Kane

In 1940, Orson Welles was best known for his work in radio, but that year George Schaefer offered him a contract to make two movies for RKO Radio Pictures. In fact, the deal was unusually generous, considering that Welles had never worked on a movie, let alone direct a film. The studio gave him complete control of the picture, from selecting the script to casting it, and most significant of all, signing off on the final cut. According to Welles, without the control the contract with RKO offered him, "I would never have made *Citizen Kane*. That's why I got that contract with Final Cut. Because George Schaefer didn't know any better! None of the other guys would have given me a contract like that."

Welles in 1941

With this contract in hand, Welles packed himself and most of the other members of the

Mercury Theater troupe off to Hollywood and began planning for his first big picture, based on the short story *Heart of Darkness* by Joseph Conrad. He laid out all his plans for the film, only to have RKO veto it because it would be too expensive to make. They also nixed *The Smiler with the Knife* because they did not feel that Welles' choice of Lucille Ball for the lead was a good idea.

As is often the case, the third time was the charm. RKO agreed to have Welles make *Citizen Kane*, and Welles co-wrote the script with Herman J Mankiewicz, a writer for the former Mercury Theater (which was now known as The Campbell Playhouse after Campbell's sponsored it). In *The Making of Citizen Kane*, author Robert Carringer noted, "Welles's first step toward the realization of Citizen Kane was to seek the assistance of a screenwriting professional. Fortunately, help was near at hand. . . . When Welles moved to Hollywood, it happened that a veteran screenwriter, Herman Mankiewicz, was recuperating from an automobile accident and between jobs ... Mankiewicz was an expatriate from Broadway who had been writing for films for almost fifteen years."

Welles would go on to produce, direct and star in the film, which was loosely based on the life of newspaper magnet William Randolph Hearst but hinted at Hearst's own life enough that the newspaper magnate famously banned all mention of the movie in his newspapers. Though Welles was criticized for his unkind treatment of the lead female character, which was also based in part on Hearst's mistress, Marion Davies, the fault for that particular piece of film history lies with Mankiewicz. He had once been close friends with Davies and gathered much of his background for the film from her gossip about her life with Hearst, but the two had a falling out, and Mankiewicz chose to take out his anger in how he portrayed the Davies character in the film.

Mankiewicz

While people often associate *Citizen Kane* with Hearst, Welles also based the character on the newspaper publisher and founder of the famous literary prize, Joseph Pulitzer, as well as the mysterious millionaire recluse Howard Hughes. He was also influenced in his writing by Conrad's *Heart of Darkness*. In reference to being asked about the people who influenced the character of Kane, Welles explained, "I'd been nursing an old notion – the idea of telling the same thing several times – and showing exactly the same thing from wholly different points of view. Basically, the idea Rashomon used later on. Mank liked it, so we started searching for the man it was going to be about. Some big American figure – couldn't be a politician, because you'd have to pinpoint him. Howard Hughes was the first idea. But we got pretty quickly to the press lords." In addition to Hearst, Pulitzer, and Hughes, Welles was also inspired in his writing by his own life. For instance, Kane's early childhood is similar to Welles', including being turned over to a guardian. All in all, it's hard to say how many different figures from American history influenced the development of Charles Foster Kane.

Once Welles was finished with the script, he felt that it was a masterpiece worthy of the best technicians and actors that Hollywood had to offer. Rumor got around about what he was doing and people began to flock to him, wanting to be part of the picture. He had his choice of film crew, and he used it well. As far as the cast was concerned, he mostly picked people he had worked with in the Mercury Theater. He encouraged their input in the film, but he still moved at lightning speed, completing the shooting in just 10 weeks. Though he was a novice, Welles studied enough to quickly become an expert, and he explained how he went about directing *Kane*: "As it turned out, the first day I ever walked onto a set was my first day as a director. I'd learned whatever I knew in the projection room — from [John] Ford. After dinner every night for about a month, I'd run *Stagecoach*, often with some different technician or department head from the studio, and ask questions. 'How was this done?' 'Why was this done?' It was like going to school."

Even as the movie was still being worked on, rumors were swirling around the movie, and the twisted, almost incestuous family tree of Hollywood actors and actresses was shaking at every branch. For example, Mankiewicz gave a copy of the script to a friend of his, Charles Lederer, who was not only Marion Davies' nephew but was also now married to the former Virginia Welles. She was still angry at her ex-husband for his infidelity and was happy to have a chance to undermine his career. Hollywood gossip columnist Hedda Hopper heard the rumors and made it a point to attend the preview screening of the movie. She immediately reported back that the film was obviously based on Hearst's life, and he in turn began a battle to keep it from ever being shown. Not only did Hearst forbid his own media outlets from showing the film, but he also began to make calls to various people in Hollywood, sharing with them some of the secrets he knew about their lives that he had not published. Studio heads throughout the town were nervous, and they put together money to try to pay off RKO, offering them enough cash to get back every dime they had invested in the film if they would just surrender the negatives and prints to them. Having seen the film, and knowing its value, RKO refused and went ahead and released it at limited venues.

Although Hearst wasn't the only source for Kane, the depiction of Kane made clear how much damage could be done to Hearst's reputation, as one of his own biographers explained, "Welles' Kane is a cartoon-like caricature of a man who is hollowed out on the inside, forlorn, defeated, solitary because he cannot command the total obedience, loyalty, devotion, and love of those around him. Hearst, to the contrary, never regarded himself as a failure, never recognized defeat, never stopped loving Marion or his wife. He did not, at the end of his life, run away from the world to entomb himself in a vast, gloomy art-choked hermitage. Orson Welles may have been a great filmmaker, but he was neither a biographer nor a historian." Ironically, Welles claimed to cut something from the film that was a more explicit reference to Hearst, saying, "In the original script we had a scene based on a notorious thing Hearst had done, which I still cannot repeat for publication. And I cut it out because I thought it hurt the film and wasn't in keeping with Kane's character. If I'd kept it in, I would have had no trouble with Hearst. He wouldn't have dared admit it was him."

Hearst

Welles also tried to disassociate the character of Susan from Davies, which may have irked Hearst most of all: "That Susan was Kane's wife and Marion was Hearst's mistress is a difference more important than might be guessed in today's changed climate of opinion. The wife was a puppet and a prisoner; the mistress was never less than a princess. Hearst built more than one castle, and Marion was the hostess in all of them: they were pleasure domes indeed, and the Beautiful People of the day fought for invitations. Xanadu was a lonely fortress, and Susan was quite right to escape from it. The mistress was never one of Hearst's possessions: he was always her suitor, and she was the precious treasure of his heart for more than 30 years, until his last breath of life. Theirs is truly a love story. Love is not the subject of *Citizen Kane*."

As bad as his financial woes were, Hearst was so bitter about *Citizen Kane*, which was released on May 1, 1941, that even before its release, Hearst fought with all his money and power to prevent its release. He would go so far as to bring FBI Director J. Edgar Hoover into the fray. Journalist Jon Wiener explained, "The F.B.I. opened its file on Welles in 1941, just after the completion of his film Citizen Kane, when Hearst was using all the power he could command to block release of the thinly disguised biography of the antilabor publisher. (It has since been acclaimed as perhaps the greatest U.S. film.) ...the Hearst press began describing Welles as a 'communist' at that point, first in a review of Welles's Broadway play *Native Son*.... Hearst's Journal American called it 'propaganda that seems closer to Moscow than Harlem.' The F.B.I. file contains forty-two pages on the play, including accusatory clips from Hearst papers. Two weeks later, when Welles's new radio series with the Free Company premiered--the group included such well-known subversives as poet Archibald MacLeish and fiction writer Sherwood Anderson, poet Stephen Vincent Benet and actor and musical writer George M. Cohan--the Hearst press called it 'communistic' and 'subversive.' A headline declared that Welles 'helps Reds.'...Hearst's critique of Welles's politics occupies a prominent place in the F.B.I. file. Citizen Kane is described there as 'inspired by [Welles's] close associations with communists over a period of years' and as 'nothing more than an extension of the Communist Party's campaign to smear one of its most effective and consistent opponents in the United States.' The file declares that 'the most intensive and extensive campaign which the Communist Party has conducted throughout its entire history has been its anti-Hearst campaign.'"

While Hearst was able to prevent many theaters in the nation from showing the movie, he could not keep critics away, and they wrote raving reviews that were lapped up by the public. *The New York Times* critic said the movie "comes close to being the most sensational film ever made in Hollywood" and continued, "Count on Mr. Welles: he doesn't do things by halves. ... Upon the screen he discovered an area large enough for his expansive whims to have free play. And the consequence is that he has made a picture of tremendous and overpowering scope, not in physical extent so much as in its rapid and graphic rotation of thoughts. Mr. Welles has put upon the screen a motion picture that really moves. As critic James Agate noted in his review, "*Citizen Kane* has entirely ousted the war as conversation fodder. Waiters ask me what I think of it, and the post is full of it. ... You know now that all the vulgar beef, beer and tobacco barons are vulgar because when they were about seven years of age somebody came and took away their skates. That is one explanation of this alleged world-shaking masterpiece, *Citizen Kane*. Another point of view is that *Citizen Kane* is so great a masterpiece that it doesn't need explaining. ... In the meantime I continue to steer a middle course. I regard Citizen Kane as a quite good film which tries to run the psychological essay in harness with your detective thriller, and doesn't quite succeed."

Gradually, one theater after another decided that they had more to lose by not showing *Citizen Kane* than by screening it. Although it's still critically acclaimed and widely recognized as one of Hollywood's greatest movies, the movie was not a financial success because too many theaters refused to show it, and those that did were often shocked by the results. *Citizen Kane* was too different from any other film at that time to be well accepted, and many people walked out in the middle of the movie, with some of them even asking for their money back. Welles later recalled, "For a couple of years after Kane, every time I walked in the streets in New York they shouted at me, 'Hey! What the hell is that movie of yours about? What does it mean?' Not, 'What is Rosebud?' but always 'what does it mean?'"

Regardless of the financial success, or lack thereof, the movie was nominated for nine Academy Awards, with Welles receiving four nominations for acting, writing, directing and producing the movie. Though he only won one of these, for Best Original Screenplay (an award shared with Mankiewicz), he was still thrilled with the film, even though RKO chose to put *Citizen Kane* in storage, perhaps in hopes that time would improve its popularity. The style in which the narrative progressed was clearly in line with Welles' opinion on what made a director good: "I want to give the audience a hint of a scene. No more than that. Give them too much and they won't contribute anything themselves. Give them just a suggestion and you get them working with you. That's what gives the theater meaning: when it becomes a social act."

Ultimately, RKO would not release it again until 1956, and by then, movies were seen more as an artistic medium than they had been in the early '40s. Young people, particularly the more sophisticated college students springing up on American campuses, flocked to see and talk about the film, and even today, it is still considered essential viewing for anyone interested in movie history. At the end of the 20th century, the American Film Institute named it the greatest movie Hollywood ever made.

While *Citizen Kane* was not literally autobiographical, it was philosophically autobiographical in that it reflected Welles' moral perspective on life, as noted by one of the more famous quotes in the movie: "The trouble is, you don't realize you're talking to two people. As Charles Foster Kane, who has 82,634 shares of Public Transit Preferred. You see, I do have a general idea of my holdings. I sympathize with you. Charles Foster Kane is a scoundrel. His paper should be run out of town. A committee should be formed to boycott him. You may, if you can form such a committee, put me down for a contribution of $1,000 dollars. On the other hand, I am the publisher of the Inquirer! As such, it's my duty - and I'll let you in on a little secret, it's also my pleasure - to see to it that decent, hard-working people in this community aren't robbed blind by a pack of money-mad pirates just because - they haven't anybody to look after their interests."

Like most of the United States, the Hearst Corporation began recovering from the Depression during World War II, and with Americans more interested than ever in daily news reports concerning the war, readership skyrocketed. At the same time, thanks to the mobilization brought about by the war, Americans had more disposable income and companies began spending more to advertise their goods to customers.

Hearst spent most of the war years at Wyntoon, and when the war was over, he returned to San Simeon and continued his building projects. He also returned to collecting art and antiques, though never again on the previous scale. As he grew older and came to grips with his own mortality, he began giving away many of his pieces, including donating some of them to the Los Angeles County Museum of Art.

With the war over but patriotism still at a fevered pitch, Hearst became particularly interested in promoting the stories of the nation in his publications. In 1945, he wrote to J. D. Gortatowsky, the president of King Features, concerning a new comic strip the company was developing: "I have had numerous suggestions for incorporating some American history of a vivid kind in the adventure strips of the comic section. The difficulty is to find something that will sufficiently interest the kids…. Perhaps a title 'Trained by Fate' would be general enough. Take Paul Revere and show him as a boy making as much of his boyhood life as possible, and culminate, of course, with his ride. Take Betsy Ross for a heroine, or Barbara Fritchie…for the girls."

His work on this project was among his last efforts. In 1947, he turned one last time to building, this time purchasing a mansion in Beverly Hills for $120,000. It sat on nearly 4 acres of land just three blocks from the famous Sunset Strip. To the Hearst family, it was known as the Beverly House. With three swimming pools, a nightclub, a movie theater on site, and tennis courts, the 29 bedroom home was, at one time, the most expensive private residence in the United States, with an estimated value of more than $165 million. Hearst lived the last three years of his life in that house, dying there on August 14, 1951. He was 88.

According to his obituary, published in the *Los Angeles Times*, "Mr. Hearst had been ill several years. Frequent reports of the serious condition of his health had caused concern throughout the Hearst domain. But the Chief, as he was known to the 27,000 workers of the various Hearst enterprises, rallied repeatedly to resume his active role as editorial head of his national chain of newspapers. Yesterday, however, he lapsed into a coma from which he did not awaken. Death came peacefully."

While all five of his sons were with him at his death, his wife Millicent had remained "at her home at Southampton, N.Y., where she was spending the summer. She said through a spokesman that she would leave for California last night for his funeral…Mr. Hearst's body was taken to the Pierce Bros. Beverly Hills Mortuary and later removed and flown to his native San Francisco. There, it is understood, he is to be buried in Cypress Lawn Cemetery where his father, Sen. George Hearst, and his mother, Mrs. Phoebe Apperson Hearst, are buried. Funeral arrangements will be announced at a later date. The Los Angeles County Board of Supervisors and the City Council adjourned yesterday out of respect to the memory of Mr. Hearst. On orders of Mayor Bowron, the City Hall Flag was lowered to half staff."

Speaking on behalf of the city, Bowron said, "The people of our city have suffered a great loss. To hundreds of thousands of people in every walk of life, William Randolph Hearst was a great and true friend. … He was for a greater Southwest, a greater California, a greater Los Angeles. He was a constant and vigilant foe of corruption and deceit. We have lost a great crusader, a man who loved his country, a man who loved our city and its people."

In spite of his many moral lapses, Cardinal Francis Spellman said of the Catholic Hearst, "I mourn the death of a great American patriot…who fought battles on many fronts for all that America signifies and who leaves to posterity traditions to continue the fight for freedom and justice that will encourage and inspire Americans for many generations."

Finally, the president of the *United Press Associations* stated that "one of the great figures of journalism has gone from among us. But the newspaper empire he created lives as a memorial to his genius. William Randolph Hearst originated many of the forms of daily publishing which now are familiar to all, and introduced an era of intense competition which ever since has had a stimulating effect on the enterprise and ingenuity of newspapering. His life and career are a conspicuous part of the history of our times."

People in Hearst's lifetime had different takes on his life and career, and he continues to have a mixed legacy, but everyone can certainly agree that Hearst was conspicuous.

The Millstone

"The director is simply the audience. So the terrible burden of the director is to take the place of that yawning vacuum, to be the audience and to select from what happens during the day which movement shall be a disaster and which a gala night. His job is to preside over accidents." – Orson Welles

In some ways, *Citizen Kane* proved to be a millstone around Welles' neck, especially over time when it became clear that he had already made the best movie of his life at the age of 26. Still, he was not one to naval gaze to write too much about what could not be changed. Instead, as someone once said, "he spent the rest of his life being Orson Welles."

Of course, he did not know right away that he his career had already peaked. In 1942, the United States was at war, and *Citizen Kane* was safely stored away on a shelf at RKO studios. Welles wanted to make another film, but the industry could not figure out what to do with him. His next movie, *The Magnificent Ambersons* (1942), was critically popular, but it ended up being so long that RKO wanted cuts made to it. It also went over budget, making it a financial disappointment. Welles later complained, "They destroyed 'Ambersons,'…'it' destroyed me." In reference to the substantial cuts made to the film, he explained, "You see, the basic intention was to portray a golden world — almost one of memory — and then show what it turns into. Having set up this dream town of the 'good old days,' the whole point was to show the automobile wrecking it — not only the family but the town. All this is out. What's left is only the first six reels. Then there's a kind of arbitrary bringing back down the curtain by a series of clumsy, quick devices. The bad, black world was supposed to be too much for people. My whole third act is lost because of all the hysterical tinkering that went on. And it was hysterical. Everybody they could find was cutting it."

Welles also took some grief for the way he introduced the actors in the movie by reading their names, as well as his own. He explained, "I got a lot of hell because of that. People think it's egotistic. The truth is, I was just speaking to a public who knew me from the radio in a way they were used to hearing on our shows. In those days we had an enormous public — in the millions — who heard us every week, so it didn't seem pompous to end a movie in our radio style."

After the slow pace of *The Magnificent Ambersons* cost them money, RKO renegotiated Welles' contract before he made his next picture, *Journey Into Fear*. RKO was determined that this film should not go over time or over budget, so they rushed filming and production, leading to a less than satisfactory outcome. At the same time, Nelson Rockefeller, then a member of the Board of Directors for RKO, approached Welles about making a documentary to promote the federal government's Good Neighbor Policy. This was considered an important part of the war effort, as it was designed to discourage South American countries from joining the Axis powers in the war. Welles was happy to comply, but it did cut into his time and effort on both *The Magnificent Ambersons* and *Journey Into Fear*, which in turn caused further problems with both movies.

The documentary, called *It's All True*, began with a budget of $1 million, half of it supplied by the United States government. Originally designed to be a colorful tale of the Rio's Carnaval, it took on a deeper meaning when Welles included the story of four poor fisherman who traveled over 1500 miles by raft to speak to Brazilian President Vargas. RKO felt that Welles was spending too much of the half million dollars they had put up and began to try to limit his production. As a result, the movie was never completed.

By the time he returned to the United States, Welles' reputation for moviemaking was pretty much shot as a result of his three most recent failures. As a result, he returned to radio, taking on two weekly series for CBS. The first, called Hello Americans, was built around his trip to Brazil, and the other, Ceiling Unlimited, was sponsored by Lockheed and was basically a red, white and blue tribute to all the great work they were doing in wartime aviation. Hello Americans was cut after a few months, and Welles was replaced by Joseph Cotten in Ceiling Unlimited.

Finding himself at loose ends, Welles spent the next few months doing guest roles on variety shows and supporting the American war effort. He also got married again, this time to famous actress Rita Hayworth. Their marriage would be stormy and ended in 1948, when their daughter, Rebecca, was still a toddler. He would later reflect on their marriage, "I loved her, yeah. Very much. But… she had become so – such a figure of lust, and she just wanted to be a housewife. … And then she had been so wonderful to me, absolutely wonderful. When I almost died of hepatitis, she spent five months with me while I recovered. And she never did anything except take care of me. When I said to her, 'I want to give up the movies and theater. Will you do that with me?' She said, 'Yes.'"

Hayworth

However, their marriage ended badly, just like his relationships with other women. Musing about this later, Welles added, "Women are another race. They're like the moon, always changing. You can only win by being the cool center of their being. You have to represent something solid and loving. The anchor. Even if you're not. You can't tell them the truth. You have to lie and play games. I've never in my entire life been with someone with whom I didn't have to play a game. I've never been with someone with whom I could be exactly who I am." Given such an attitude, his problems with women make more sense.

Though he was no longer directing, Welles continued to act, starring opposite Joan Fontaine in 1944's *Jane Eyre*, and he also played a small part in *All for the Boys*, performing a magic act that included sawing Marlene Dietrich in half. Later that year, he began work on a new radio show entitled Orson Welles' Almanac, but that series was short-lived, as was the Mercury Wonder Show, broadcast from military bases around the world.

After the war, Welles again tried his hand at directing. This time, the movie was called *The Stranger*, which followed the efforts of Edward G. Robinson to hunt down a Nazi war criminal living in the U.S. The movie did well financially and opened the door for Welles to make more pictures, but when he made *Around the World*, a musical version of Jules Verne's *Around the World In 80 Days*, the show's failure put Welles in a financial bind that drove him back to radio.

His next two shows, CBS's The Mercury Summer Theatre On the Air and ABC's Orson Welles Commentaries, were also poorly received, so Welles returned to Hollywood to make *The Lady from Shanghai* for Columbia Pictures. Not only was Welles forced to work with his soon-to-be ex-wife Rita Hayworth in the film, but he and Harry Cohn, the producer, locked horns on how the film should be edited. Cohn thought it was too dark and insisted that it be reshot, yet even after that, he also cut out nearly an hour of Welles' work. What remained was both a box office disaster and a classic film noir, leaving one critic to call it "the weirdest great movie ever made." Orson's own daughter Chris, who was often on the set of the movie despite still being young, later talked about the making of the movie:

> "I couldn't recognize Rita, because her lovely auburn tresses had disappeared and instead she had this short bleached blonde hair. I said, 'Rita what happened to your beautiful hair?' She said, 'Well, in this movie I'm doing with Orsie,' (that's what Rita called Orson), 'I have to be this cold, evil person, so Orsie cut off my hair, to make me look different.' Well I had a hard time imaging that Rita could be cold and evil and I think the public, who adored her and saw her as a love goddess, shared my reaction. She had just played in *Gilda*, and one of her famous remarks was 'men go to bed with Gilda but in the morning they wake up with me.' I don't think they ever forgave my father for cutting off her hair and for turning her into a murderess. So the public didn't like her new look. Who knows, maybe that's why The Lady From Shanghai was not the popular success that my father wanted. It was his dream to make a box-office hit. He thought if only he could make a box-office hit, maybe he would be more accepted in Hollywood, yet it seems that everything he did turned into art. He was like King Midas, who turned everything he touched to gold. Whatever my father made it somehow ended up being very arty, or different and strange, so very often the public didn't really understand it."

Determined to bring in his next film under budget, Welles had his cast pre-record the soundtrack for Republic Pictures' *Macbeth*, and in this version, Welles interpreted Macbeth as a clash between the old, pagan face of Europe and new Christian ideas. Film experts have since observed that of all the movies Welles made after *Citizen Kane*, this *Macbeth* is the one most similar to his earlier triumph, but when it opened, the American public and the critics were not impressed. Leaving for Europe, Welles left the film in the hands of a subordinate to rework.

While in Europe, he starred as Harry Lime in *The Third Man* (1949), and he enjoyed the opportunity to play alongside his old friend Joseph Cotten, who he had worked with in *Citizen Kane* as well. However, he was shocked to see how different work in other countries was from that in the United States, observing, "… how theater actors manage to get along in Spain I don't know, because they do two shows a night. Same thing in a lot of Latin American countries, still – two shows a night. I had a friend who… had to finish a movie he was making. And he said, 'I've got this show. And if I close it, I'll never get it open again with any business. Will you do it? What will you take?' And I said, 'I'll do it for free.' So for a week I did his show, while he finished his movie, but there were two performances a night. And at the end of that week, I didn't know how I – or he – lived through it.

The Third Man ended up being a hit all over Europe and America, so Welles kept at it when he returned to America. In 1950, he appeared with Tyrone Power in *Prince of Foxes*, and later in *The Black Rose*, again with Power, in 1950. At the same time, Welles threw his energy and any money that he made from acting into a film version of *Othello*, which was filmed all over Europe and Morocco between 1949 and 1951. It premiered at the Cannes Film Festival in 1952 and immediately won the Palme d'Or, the festival's highest award. Meanwhile, Welles worked for a year as the host and narrator of *The Black Museum*, a crime drama based on tales from Scotland Yard's own records.

Harry Alan Towers, the producer of *The Black Museum*, liked Welles' work and hired him again in 1953 to play Professor Moriarty in *The Adventures of Sherlock Holmes*. Later that year, Welles returned to America just long enough to star in a live broadcast of *King Lear*, premiering on CBS on October 18.

In 1954, Welles starred in several radio broadcast roles, including that of Lord Mountdrago in Three Cases Of Murder. He also appeared with Forrest Tucker in Trouble in the Green. Then, John Huston, an old friend, cast him in *Moby Dick*, but even though he was barely 40 years old, Welles was morbidly obese and no longer suited for the role of a swarthy ship captain. Instead, he played Father Mapple opposite of Gregory Peck.

By this time, Welles had also begun work as the director of his next film, *Mr. Arkadin*, and he also starred in the title role as a millionaire trying to get in touch with a mysterious past. Though he had only a limited budget with which to make the film, Welles insisted on filming it on location in several European countries. Welles' leading lady was Paola Mori, the daughter of an

Italian aristocrat, whom he married shortly after filming concluded, but the same problems that had pestered him before continued to dog Welles, as the producer felt that he was moving too slowly in the editing process and eventually fired him.

Welles arriving in Madrid to work on Mr. Arkadin in 1954

When Welles and Mori married in 1955, she was already pregnant with their only child, a daughter born on November 13 of that year named Beatrice, after Orson's mother. However, and by now not surprisingly, Welles and Mori didn't remain close very long. She was a devout Catholic, so the two never divorced, but they lived apart for the rest of their lives.

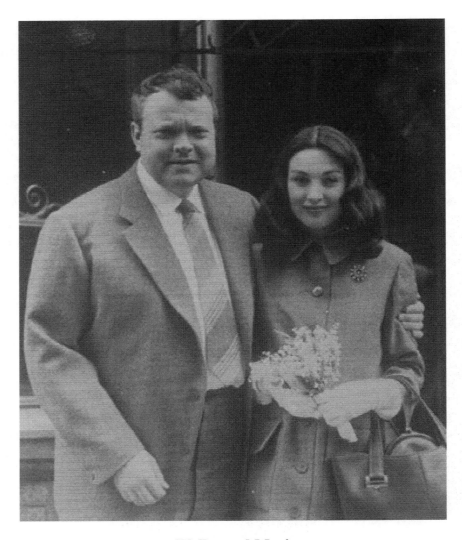

Welles and Mori

Welles had already dabbled in television, which was becoming more popular by the day, so he directed two television series for the British Broadcasting Company. The first, the Orson Welles Sketchbook, featured 15 minute segments of Welles drawling on camera while reminiscing about his past work, which didn't sound titillating and only lasted six shows. The second series, Around the World with Orson Welles, also lasted only six episodes, with each one being a traveler's look at cities around Europe. During each episode, Welles acted as both interviewer and host, filling in facts and personal observations from his own travels.

Welles in 1960

By the end of 1956, Welles had returned to Hollywood, where he filled his time doing guest spots for radio shows. One of the most interesting of these was called Tomorrow, a drama built around a potential nuclear holocaust funded and produced by the Federal Civil Defense Administration. Welles also made a comical guest appearance on *I Love Lucy*, the most popular television show during that period, which in turn led to him filming a pilot for her company, Desilu Productions. Though it did not air until 1958, the film, entitled *The Fountain of Youth*, won a Peabody Award that year.

In 1958, Welles began work on *Touch of Evil*, a film based on Witt Masterson's novel *Badge of Evil*. Welles starred opposite Charlton Heston, and he was also able to recruit a number of actors and crew members that he worked with in the past, including Maurice Cyberman (from *Citizen Kane*) and Marlene Dietrich. For one of the few times in his life, Welles completed the project on schedule and within budget, but in spite of their initial enthusiasm, the studio still insisted on reworking a number of important themes in the film. In response, Welles sent the studio a memo numbering 58 pages outlining his problems with what they had done and offering to help them correct them. Naturally, the studio wasn't terribly interested in that form of help and eventually cut another 30 minutes from the movie before they finally released it. This time, the work done by the higher-ups seemingly paid off, as the movie opened to rave reviews across Europe before going on to win the top award at the Brussels World Fair.

Welles in *Touch of Evil*

Welles made two more films in Hollywood before he returned to Europe, where he began work on his next project, *Don Quixote*, filming it on location in Spain and Italy. But before he could even finish the film, he began work as director for *David and Goliath*, which included starring as King Saul. From there, he moved on to Hong Kong to star in *Ferry to Hong Kong*, then headed to Paris to make *Crack in the Mirror*, and then Yugoslavia to film *Battle of Neretva*. All the while, he was still trying to get *Don Quixote* completed. Though he would finish shooting it, he would never finish editing it to his own satisfaction, and in fact, he almost changed the entire format of the movie, just to get it finished. He told a friend, "I wanted to finally get it done, with the title *When Are You Going to Finish Don Quixote?* That would be the name of the movie. And it would be all about Spain, a country I've known since I was a boy. What's happened to it, and why Quixote is still important. That film would be much more expensive…because I'd need to shoot footage in modern Spain. You know, de-Francoed Spain. But how to sell Quixote…? It's hard if you haven't got in the door…"

Eventually, Welles made eight half-hours episodes of a short lived television series called *In the Land of Don Quixote*, which in many ways was an Italian version of his American series, Around the World With Orson Welles. This time, however, Welles made the show more family friendly, featuring his wife and daughter in the episodes. Fluent in Italian, Welles felt that he should narrate the show himself, but the network disagreed, pointing out that he still had a very American accent. They kept putting off airing the show until 1964, by which time they had had the narration dubbed in by a native Italian.

In 1962, Welles began work on *The Trial*, based on the novel by Franz Kafka, who he admired as a writer: "In my reading of the book — and my reading is probably more wrong than a lot of people's — I see the monstrous bureaucracy which is the villain of the piece as not only Kafka's clairvoyant view of the future, but his racial and cultural background of being occupied by the Austro-Hungarian Empire…I wanted a 19th century look for a great deal of what would be, in fact, expressionistic."

The Trial, his own personal favorite among his later pictures, starred Anthony Perkins as the main character, and Welles' wife Paola was also in the movie, as well as a number of other up-and-coming stars. Without money to build sets, he instead shot the film in an abandoned French railway station. The completed work turned out to be everything he had hoped for, and even much of what he needed at this point in his life. He once said, "What made it possible for me to make the picture is that I've had recurring nightmares of guilt all my life: I'm in prison and I don't know why — going to be tried and I don't know why. It's very personal for me. A very personal expression, and it's not all true that I'm off in some foreign world that has no application to myself; it's the most autobiographical movie that I've ever made, the only one that's really close to me. And just because it doesn't speak in a Middle Western accent doesn't mean a damn thing. It's much closer to my own feelings about everything than any other picture I've ever made."

Unfortunately, The Trial failed at the box office, and critics panned it too, accusing Welles of again making the same kind of movie he always made. Even 20 years later, he remained sensitive about the film, grousing, "Exactly, I repeated myself. I believe we do it all the time. We always take up certain elements again. How can it be avoided? An actor's voice always has the same timbre and, consequently, he repeats himself. It is the same for a singer, a painter…There are always certain things that come back, for they are part of one's personality, of one's style. If these things didn't come into play, a personality would be so complex that it would become impossible to identify it. It is not my intention to repeat myself, but in my work there should certainly be references to what I have done in the past. Say what you will, but *The Trial* is the best film I ever made…I have never been so happy as when I made this film."

With his career seemingly going up and down at any given time, throughout the remainder of the 1960s, Welles took on whatever acting or directing work he could find. In 1966, he began work on *Chimes at Midnight*, considered by some to be one of his best films. Based on the play Five Kings, which Welles had written and produced in the later 1930s, it combines elements of five Shakespearean plays to tell the story of the rise to power of the early Tudors. Welles himself plays Falstaff, a man who has an on-again off-again relationship with the future Henry V, known through most of the film as "Prince Hal." Famous film critic Robert Ebert once wrote,

"Welles was born to play Falstaff, not only because of the physical similarity but because of the rich voice, sonorous and amused, and the shared life experience. Both men lived long and too well, were at odds with the powers at court and were constantly in debt. Both knew disappointment, and one of the most sublime moments in Welles' career is simply the expression on his face at the coronation of Henry V, when he cries out 'God save thee, my sweet boy,' and the new king replies, 'I know thee not, old man.'"

The film was well received critically and nominated for many award, including the Palme d'Or, and though it did not win, the Cannes committee still recognized its importance with an honorary prize. For his part, Welles once said that the movie was so good, "If I wanted to get into heaven on the basis of one movie, that's the one I'd offer up."

In fact, as Welles got older and his health deteriorated, he began to think more about getting into heaven. He had never been a religious man in the traditional sense of the word, but he did believe that everyone ought to believe in something, saying, "I have a great love and respect for religion, great love and respect for atheism. What I hate is agnosticism, people who do not choose." When he was asked about his faith in 1982, he joked with Merv Griffin "I try to be a Christian, I don't pray really, because I don't want to bore God." On the other hand, he did not shy away from religiously themed movies. He provided the narration for 1961's *King of Kings* and had a small but well respected part as Cardinal Wolsey in *A Man for All Seasons*. However, he shied away from making explicitly religious pictures for the same reason he shied away from making explicitly sexual ones, saying, "I hate it when people pray on the screen. It's not because I hate praying, but whenever I see an actor fold his hands and look up in the spotlight, I'm lost. There's only one other thing in the movies I hate as much, and that's sex. You just can't get in bed or pray to God and convince me on the screen."

Welles claimed to have some sort of Christian faith, though he also occasionally mentioned that he might be Jewish on his father's side. Both faiths definitely influenced both his business and his politics. During the mid-1980s he observed, "In common with all Protestant or Jewish cultures, America was developed on the idea that your word is your bond. Otherwise, the frontier could never have opened, because it was lawless. A man's word had to mean something. My theory is that everything went to hell with Prohibition, because it was a law nobody could obey. So the whole concept of the rule of law was corrupted at that moment. Then came Vietnam, and marijuana, which clearly shouldn't be illegal, but is. If you go to jail in Texas for ten years when you light up a joint, who are you? You're a lawbreaker. It's just like Prohibition was. When people accept breaking the law is normal, something happens to the whole society. You see?"

On the other hand, he clearly didn't let a sense of traditional Christian values regarding sex and marriage influence his behavior. While working on *The Trial*, Welles met and fell in love with Oja Kodar, a Croatian actress he cast to star in the film. They began seeing each other romantically in 1962, but Welles broke their relationship off when Mori told him she might have cancer. He moved back home and lived with her for another three years. In the meantime,

Kodar moved to Paris and became romantically involved with another young actor. Three years passed before Welles learned where she had moved to, but when he did, he charged over to her Parisian hotel room, busted down the door, and presented the startled Kodar with a love letter he had been carrying with him for three years. Needless to say, this won her heart, and though he would remain married to Mori, the rest of his romantic life was devoted to Kodar.

Welles and Kodar

In 1969, Welles gave permission for a small movie house in Cambridge, Massachusetts to be named The Orson Welles Cinema. This is perhaps reflective of his pessimistic view of the future of films, a concern he once gave voice to: "I rather think the cinema will die. Look at the energy being exerted to revive it -- yesterday it was color, today three dimensions. I don't give it forty years more. Witness the decline of conversation. Only the Irish have remained incomparable conversationalists, maybe because technical progress has passed them by. " In spite of his concerns, Welles was supportive of his namesake establishment and even visited in person in 1977.

1969 also proved to be the last year Welles would live overseas. He was concerned personally over tabloid stories being published in Europe about his relationship with Kodar, because even though he was devoted to her romantically, he did not want to upset or embarrass Moir by letting their affair become public knowledge. Professionally, he was also being offered several appealing roles in television shows and movies, so in 1970 he gave up on Don Quixote, moved back to Los Angeles and accepted a role in *The Kremlin Letter*, a new film being directed by his old friend John Huston.

Once back in the U.S., Welles wasted no time jumping into the political fray. Later in 1970, he narrated a satire of the Nixon administration entitled the *Begetting of the President*, and whenever possible, Welles used the money he earned from working for other people to finance his own projects. He also used his popularity on the talk show circuit to promote his work and to attract backers. For many years, hardly a week went by that Welles wasn't on Johnny Carson, Merv Griffin or some other entertaining talk show.

Welles' last large scale project was *The Other Side of the Wind*, which he worked on throughout the early 1970s. Semi-autobiographical, it tells the story of a washed up director who is trying to raise funds to create his final big production, and like the main character, Welles was unable to complete this picture because of lack of funds. The only other film in which he appeared during 1970 was *Louis XVIII of France*, in which he portrayed the aging title character. That same year, he provided humorous narration for Start the Revolution Without Me, a comedy poking gentle fun at America's revolutionary beginnings.

In 1971, Welles received an honorary award from the Academy of Motion Picture Arts and Sciences in recognition of his "superlative artistry and versatility in the creation of motion pictures". Unwilling to attend the award ceremony in person, Welles asked John Huston to accept it on his behalf, and Huston used his acceptance speech as an opportunity to chide the academy, saying, "Genius is a word that must be used very sparingly, especially in this world of films. Those who claim it who don't have and others who do have it keep the fact concealed for fear of being called difficult, which usually translates as unemployable. So at one time or another, Orson Welles has been considered both difficult and unemployable, I know too damn well. But from the very first…Welles' mastery of the medium was evident. Unfortunately, only once, in *Kane*, was he free to exercise his talents without restraint. Subsequent productions were cut by other hands or, like his *Macbeth* made on impossibly low budgets. Yet in every picture he ever made his brilliance shown through."

In 1973, Welles completed his last great picture, *F for Fake*, which told the story of the famous art forger Elmyr de Hory. He built his script around a documentary that had already been completed in France, and he cast Oja Kodar and Joseph Cotten in the lead. To promote the film, Welles made a five-minute long trailer, complete with topless shots of Kodar, which ensured the trailer was banned in America. American viewers showed little interest in the film anyway.

Perhaps because of his advancing age, Welles took this rejection particularly hard. More than a decade later, he would still recall:

> "The tragedy of my life is that I can't get the Americans to like it. Outside of New York, the critics hated it. In Chicago, Cleveland, St. Louis – they were furious with it. They seemed to think I was attacking critics. Which I wasn't, but why not? It did make fools of them. Anyway, I think, *F for Fake* is the only really original movie I've made since *Kane*. You see, everything else is only carrying movies a little further back along the same path. I believe that the movies – all say terrible thing –

have never gone beyond *Kane*. That doesn't mean that there haven't been good movies, or great movies. But everything has been down now in movies...

> Every artistic form... has only so many possibilities and so long a life. And I have a feeling that in movies, until we break completely, we are only increasing the library of good works. I know that as the director of movie actors in front of the camera, I have nowhere to move forward. I can only make another good work."

As the 1970s wore on, Welles work became more and more eclectic. First, he hosted a television series entitled Orson Welles's Great Mysteries in 1973 and 1974, which was in many ways a television version of the old Mercury Theatre, but the series was not popular with young American audiences and was cancelled after just one season. Later that year, he once more teamed up with Harry Alan Towers to provide one of the voices in his radio production of Ten Little Indians.

In 1975, Welles provided narration for the popular documentary *Bugs Bunny: Superstar*, a nostalgic tribute to one of Warner Brothers' most successful franchises. That same year, Welles received a Lifetime Achievement Award from the American Film Institute, a distinction that had only been given to two other people at the time: John Ford and James Cagney.

Ironically, Welles' popularity increased during the decade more for his past work than anything he was currently doing. During the 1970s, people were becoming increasingly interested in Welles' directorial style, especially in some of his more famous works, which led to him being asked to make documentaries on how various movies developed. The first of these documentaries was *Filming Othello*, released in 1979. Filmed in West Germany, it was shown in theaters around the world. Two years later, *Filming The Trial* opened to similar reviews.

Still, the bills had to be paid, and during the late 1970s, Welles career fell to a point where he was forced to make a living by making commercials. Fortunately, because he was Orson Welles, the companies who hired him were looking for someone to speak with dignity, not to float around in a toilet tank. Thus, Welles became the spokesman for Paul Masson Vineyards, ("We will sell no wine before its time.") and Carlsberg beer ("Probably the best lager in the world").

Orson's career actually began to pick up a bit in 1981 when he hosted a popular documentary about the famous seer Nostradamus, *The Man Who Saw Tomorrow*. The following year, the BBC contracted with him to make *The Orson Welles Story* as part of their Arena series. The broadcast featured an extensive interview with Welles, as well as people he had worked with in the past. This was followed by narration for two of Manwar's albums, *Fighting the World* and *Battle Hymns*.

During the last years of his life, Welles focused his attention on doing voice over work that would not tax his physical health. That is how the great Shakespearean actor came to be the voice of the mysterious Robin Masters in the popular television series, *Magnum P.I.*, beginning in 1979. Masters was never seen on camera but communicated primarily through phone calls to his estate, Robin's Nest. After Welles' sudden death, the character slowly faded from the program, until the lead character, Thomas Magnum, accuses another character of hiring a man "who sounds like Orson Welles" to pretend to be Masters.

As strange as it may seem that Welles ever appeared on a somewhat humorous television detective drama set in Hawaii, it is even stranger to realize that he gave voice to the robot Unicron in *The Transformers: The Movie* in 1985. He also provided an introduction to a unique, partially black and white episode of the television series *Moonlighting*. His last movie work was as narrator of Henry Jaglom's Someone to Love.

By the time he died, Welles' personal and professional affairs had become quite muddled. Beginning in 1966, he owned two houses, and his legal residence in Las Vegas was where Mori and Beatrice lived. However, Welles himself spent very little time there, telling Mori that his busy filming schedule forced him to travel. What he didn't tell her was that most of his travelling was with Kodar. In addition to living together in at times in Paris or Madrid, the two also shared a home in the Los Angeles, beginning in 1970. Amazingly, Mori never learned about her husband's secret life until 1984, just one year before his death. At that point in time, she demanded that he leave their home and never return, though the two remained somewhat friendly and regularly spoke to each other by phone.

Both the *Moonlighting* episode and *Someone to Love* were released after Welles' sudden death from a heart attack during the night of October 10, 1985. Just hours earlier he had taped what would be his final interview with Merv Griffin. True to form, just as he had been in life, Welles was controversial in death. It fell to Mori and Beatrice to plan the funeral, so they had his body cremated and planned a simple, "family only" memorial service. Their excuse was that Welles left not enough money for an elaborate funeral. Neither Kodar nor Welles' other two ex-wives were invited. His oldest daughter, Chris, later criticized their plans, saying that the service took place in a bad part of Los Angeles and that the facility, located in what "looked more like a hot sheets motel than a funeral home," "had the look of a cheap motel room." There were no flowers, music or speakers. Everyone just sat in the room looking at Welles' ashes until a frail elderly man stood up. He introduced himself as Roger Hill, Welles' 90 year old mentor from back in his Todd days. After sitting down, he looked around and then said, much too loudly, "This is awful! Awful!...Orson never wanted to be cremated. He hated the whole idea of cremation. Thank God he doesn't know what they did to him!" The one thing the family did get right was the disposal of the ashes. They sent them to Ronda, Spain, where they were placed in an old well that had been planted in flowers.

Needless to say, Welles' personal lifestyle made for a complicated estate. While he left Kodar the home they'd shared in Los Angeles and the rights to the rest of his incomplete films, he left everything else to Mori. However, she didn't like being left out of anything, so she fought the will in court. After a year of haggling, the two women finally agreed to an acceptable division of property, but in a turn of events that even Welles himself could not have imagined, Mori was killed in an automobile accident while on her way to sign the newly drawn up papers. As a result, Beatrice inherited both her mother's share of the estate, and the battle over it, a fight that continues to this day and has prevented any of his final projects from being completed.

Online Resources

Other books about 20th century American history by Charles River Editors

Other books about Hearst on Amazon

Other books about Welles on Amazon

Further Reading

Acord, David. When Mars Attacked: Orson Welles, The War of the Worlds & the Radio Broadcast That Changed America Forever (2013)

Anile, Alberto and Marcus Perryman. Orson Welles in Italy (2013)

Biskind, Peter. My Lunches with Orson: Conversations between Henry Jaglom and Orson Welles (2013)

Brady, Frank. Citizen Welles: A Biography of Orson Welles (2013)

Callow, Simon. Orson Welles: Volume 1: The Road to Xanadu (1997)

Orson Welles: Volume 2: Hello Americans (2006)

Carlson, Oliver (2007). Hearst – Lord of San Simeon. Read Books.

Davies, Marion (1975). The Times We Had: Life with William Randolph Hearst. Indianapolis: Bobbs-Merrill.

Estrin, Mark W. Orson Welles: Interviews (Conversations with Filmmakers) (2002)

Feder, Chris Welles. In My Father's Shadow: A Daughter Remembers Orson Welles (2011)

Feeney, F.X. and Paul Duncan. Orson Welles (2006)

France, Richard. The Theatre of Orson Welles (1977)

Orson Welles on Shakespeare: The W.P.A. and Mercury Theatre Playscripts (2013)

Hearst, William Randolph, Jr. (1991). The Hearsts: Father and Son. Niwot, CO: Roberts Rinehart.

Higham, Charles. Orson Welles: The Rise and Fall of an American Genius (1985)

Leaming, Barbara. Orson Welles: A Biography (2004)

Lesberg, Sandy. Orson Welles In Paris (2011)

Mcbride, Joseph. What Ever Happened to Orson Welles?: A Portrait of an Independent Career
(1975)

Orson Welles (1996)

Mereghetti, Paolo. Masters of Cinema: Orson Welles (2011)

Naremore, James. The Magic World of Orson Welles (1989)

Nasaw, David (2000). The Chief: The Life of William Randolph Hearst. Boston: Houghton
Mifflin

Orson Welles's Citizen Kane: A Casebook (Casebooks in Criticism) (2004)

Procter, Ben H. (1998). William Randolph Hearst: The Early Years, 1863–1910. New York:
Oxford University Press.

Procter, Ben H. (2007). William Randolph Hearst: The Later Years, 1911–1951. New York:
Oxford University Press.

Rosenbaum, Jonathan. Discovering Orson Welles (2007)

Swanberg, W.A. (1961). Citizen Hearst. New York: Scribner.

Tarbox, Todd. Orson Welles and Roger Hill: A Friendship in Three Acts (2013)

Thomas, François and Jean-Piere Berthomé. Orson Welles at Work (2008)

Thomson, David. Rosebud: The Story of Orson Welles (1997)

Tonguette, Peter Prescott. Orson Welles Remembered: Interviews With His Actors, Editors,
Cinematographers And Magicians (2007)

Welles, Orson, Peter Bogdanovich and Jonathan Rosenbaum. This Is Orson Welles (1998)

Orson Welles Library (2007)

Whyte, Kenneth (2009). The Uncrowned King: The Sensational Rise of William Randolph
Hearst. Berkeley: Counterpoint.Cowie, Peter. The Cinema of Orson Welles (1983)

Free Books by Charles River Editors

We have brand new titles available for free most days of the week. To see which of our titles are currently free, click on this link.

Discounted Books by Charles River Editors

We have titles at a discount price of just 99 cents everyday. To see which of our titles are currently 99 cents, click on this link.

Made in the USA
Las Vegas, NV
31 December 2020